TALKING TO RUDOLF HESS

TALKING TO RUDOLF HESS

Desmond Zwar

For my late wife, Delphine, who transcribed the Hess tapes. And often wept.
Desmond Zwar, Beechworth, Australia, 2009.

'Hitler, you know, had great respect for the British people, the British Empire and British culture and the civilisation that Britain had brought into the world ...'
Rudolf Hess, speaking from his Spandau prison cell.

First published 2010

The History Press
The Mill, Brimscombe Port
Stroud, Gloucestershire, GL5 2QG
www.thehistorypress.co.uk

© Desmond Zwar, 2010

The right of Desmond Zwar to be identified as the Author
of this work has been asserted in accordance with the
Copyrights, Designs and Patents Act 1988.

British Library Cataloguing in Publication Data.
A catalogue record for this book is available from the British Library.

ISBN 978 0 7524 5522 8

Typesetting and origination by The History Press
Printed in India by Replika Press Pvt. Ltd.
Manufacturing managed by Jellyfish Print Solutions Ltd

CONTENTS

CONTENTS

CHAPTER 1

NUDES ON HORSEBACK

I awoke on a chilly winter's morning, burrowing further under the blankets, summoning the courage to make a dash from the warm bed to the shower, when the phone rang.

'Desmond? Neil Hawkes here.' The chief of the London bureau of the Melbourne *Herald*, my old paper in Australia; a pedantic man, as always, taking his time to explain himself while I'm freezing in my pyjamas by my desk. I silently urge him to get to the point.

He had been working through the night, he said, and there had come on the teleprinter an odd message from one of the *Herald* group's stable, the *Australasian Post*. A request he obviously felt was probably a time-waster, but grudgingly he would pay me to check it out anyway. 'I'm not enthusiastic about the end result.' (Yes, yes. Get on with it!)

I knew, as he did, that the *Post* was a notorious 'tits and bums' magazine devoted to sex, Australiana, oddball stories and sport. It tended to run pictures of outback toilets and dogs with two heads. By no stretch of the imagination had it ever touched on matters intellectual; and to my knowledge had rarely shown an interest in what was going on anywhere outside Australia.

That was why the London man was so puzzled, he ruminated. The *Post's* editor desired an interview with the celebrated artist, Dame Laura Knight, the only living female Royal Academician. 'He's said something in the cable about Dame Laura painting nudes on horseback. He'll want pictures.' The penny dropped! Nudes and horses. Together! I said I'd go and see the old lady. It helped pay the rent. I dashed off to the shower. Working at the time for a lowly wage on the *Daily Mail*, I knew I had to grasp at freelance crumbs in a thin week.

Dame Laura lived alone in St John's Wood, and when I phoned, she charmingly invited me to 'take tea' with her at three o'clock the next afternoon. I took a tube train to the nearest station and walked along a beautiful terrace of houses and rang the doorbell. She came to the door: a small, greying woman in her late seventies. Greeting me with a firm handshake, she led the way upstairs to her huge, airy studio. Cuttings in the *Mail* newspaper library had said she was a painter of world rank, and that made my task more embarrassing. How was I going to ask her about naked ladies riding horses? And then arrange to have the paintings photographed for the salacious readers of the *Post*?

A Royal Doulton tea service sat ready on a tray with a plate of tiny cucumber sandwiches. 'But before we sit down, let me show you my studio,' Dame Laura said. She led me on a tour of her paintings of ballet dancers, clowns and, I noticed, circus horses. The old lady must have been stunningly attractive when she was young. She wore her hair in a plait that was wound round her head; her eyes twinkling with merriment, raising her hands in girlish joy when she laughed. In the middle of the barn-like room, gazing at a sketch of one of her ballerinas I took the plunge.

'Dame Laura, I hope you won't be offended by this, but I have been asked if you would show me your paintings of … er … naked girls on horseback.'

She looked puzzled for a brief second, then she laughed. 'Oh my boy! I am sorry to disappoint you. I paint nudes as you see and all my life I have been fascinated by circuses and have painted circus people and their horses. But never together. Have I disappointed you?'

I assured her, red-faced, that she had not. Only some prurient fellow back in Melbourne might be frustrated. We settled down to enjoy our China tea. From my place on the sofa I glanced across the studio and tried to remember where I'd seen the large painting that dominated the room. Then the penny descended in the foggy brain for the second time. It was the courtroom dock scene at the Nuremberg Trials; the line-up of the notorious accused: Hess, Goering, Von Ribbentrop, Speer. Dame Laura's eyes were twinkling again. 'You recognise it?' I assured her, yes of course I did. She was the official war artist at Nuremberg. This was one of the world's most famous paintings. 'That was my working painting,' she explained. 'The original is in the Imperial War Museum.' Nudes on horseback. I felt ill.

I explained, on the second cup of tea, that I was interested in German history. As a small boy, with a German name, I had been the butt of taunts and bashings at my country school. 'Nazi! Nazi!' I'd never forgotten the shame. We walked across to the painting. 'Look at poor Goering,' she said. 'He had a terrible cold while I was painting him.' Then, as we returned to the sofa, she said: 'You must forget about interviewing me. There is a great friend of mine who was at Nuremberg, and was ever so much more important. When he comes to London he takes tea with me and sits where you are sitting now. Colonel Burton Andrus was the Commandant of Nuremberg prison, the building next to the court where the trials were going on. His job was to keep those terrible men in their cells; to prevent people getting them out; or even murdering them; and that was a real possibility. He has never told anybody his story. Why don't you let me put you in touch with him?'

She always had her 'nap' at four o'clock. Why didn't I wait in the studio for her, and in the meantime, read the air-letters she had written from the courtroom to her husband Harold, in London? They would probably give me an idea of what the Nuremberg Trials were like. She went downstairs and returned with a bundle of the blue letters in a box. 'There,' she said. 'That will help you understand.'

I had in my hands a pile of letters that were a daily diary. They described in vivid, intimate detail what she had observed from her tiny observation box high up on one of the courtroom walls. And indeed, there at the top of one letter was her pen-picture of Goering: 'He fidgets, sniffles, wipes his nose constantly. He looks miserable,' she had told Harold. On the left-hand corner of the page there was a thumb-nail sketch of the fat, hated man, nose dripping.

By the time she came back I had made up my mind: I would contact Colonel Andrus in Tacoma, Washington, and ask him if I might discuss my writing about his Nuremberg life. The security of the *Daily Mail* had to be put to one side. Sure, the outlay of time and money would be considerable; but if he was prepared to talk for the first time about what went on in Nuremberg prison, it would be a literary scoop. The old boy sounded a character, but a formidable one. I wondered if he'd break his silence after all these years, and why he hadn't by now?

I went back to my one-room bachelor flat at Cadogan Gardens, London, and wrote to Col. Andrus. It was 11 July 1965:

> You will have had a note from Dame Laura Knight introducing me. She has spoken a lot about you … and after researching at my newspaper library at the London *Daily Mail*, I have become more intrigued than ever that you must hold the real story of Nuremberg that has never been written. I feel the real, personal story by you, of how those men lived and how you worked on their physical and mental well-being would be something people all over the world would want to read.
>
> I know this may be forward and presumptuous and I hope you are not offended …

Weeks went by and then came a two-paragraph note from Andrus. 'Maybe', he said. 'One day, maybe.' For months after my visit to Dame Laura Knight, our sporadic, mostly one-sided correspondence seemed to be destined to go nowhere. It was only when I pointed out in a final letter that he was 75 and 'history might die' with him, that I had his phone call.

3 a.m. 'Mr. Zwar? Andrus here. When ya comin' over?'

'Colonel! I can leave tomorrow.'

'Fine. Let me know what time you're gettin' into Tacoma.'

He's agreed! I'd made this accidental connection with this man surely with history in his grizzled head. He had held in custody twenty-four of the world's most evil men – Streicher, Goering, Sauckel, Funk et al., while they were being tried in Nuremberg Court, next door to his prison. I was to meet him. And only because a sex-starved Australian magazine wanted pictures of naked ladies riding horses!

Airlines operating between Britain and the US were on strike. I met Burton C. Andrus, the ex-Commandant of Nuremberg prison, after a flight to Amsterdam, another across the Atlantic to Canada, and a bus ride to Tacoma, Washington State. A stern, crew-cut, greying man with a fierce expression on a leathery face, Andrus exuded no-nonsense army. He picked me up at Tacoma bus station at the end of my long hours' travelling, and I felt exhausted. When we got into his car the colonel said he'd booked me into the visiting professorial quarters at the nearby University of Puget Sound, where he taught geography. ('Thank God! I can sleep!')

'But in the meantime, I've arranged dinner at my club.' I sighed inwardly. Bed would have been perfect.

I sat down at the Elks Club dining table, bleary-eyed from the long trip, and tentatively broached the subject of diaries. I hoped, I said, he'd still have the notes and diary records he had kept at Nuremberg. He stopped eating his steak: 'Hell no. I never kept diaries.' My stomach sank. How, then, would he remember what actually went on? There had been nothing in my London newspaper archives about the prison itself; there were cabinets full of cuttings about the trial and a whole row of books that had been written about the proceedings and the fate of the accused Nazis. But the news blackout on his prison, adjacent to where the trial was taking place, and what went on in the cells that incarcerated the Nazi leaders, had been coldly efficient. 'Yeah. I operated a tight ship,' agreed the nuggety Andrus. 'I tried to make sure nothin' got out.' Obviously nothing had.

That was why I was there, I said. I wanted – through him – to tell the world what it was like incarcerating Hitler's most notorious colleagues.

What sources were available for my research? Didn't he have files? Instructions? Letters? I had a sinking feeling that the whole project was turning into a dead end.

He grinned at me as he finished his chocolate dessert. 'Well, there's a whole lot of stuff up in my loft in tin trunks at home. But you wouldn't want to go up there in the dust. You told me in one of your letters you get hay fever.'

It was hard to know when Colonel Andrus was serious or joking. He had an immobile face and one eye that just stared at you, the other hardly moving, leaving you to make up your own mind. I said if it was okay with him, I would go up into the attic the next morning and look at the 'stuff'. And risk the hay fever.

Next day I went to his home and climbed the ladder. Lying against one side of the loft were three dusty trunks he had brought back from Nuremberg in 1946. I carefully opened each one and pulled out orderly files of documents, letters and stapled reports. As I opened them I saw Classified, Top Secret, and Eyes Only across the majority of the folders. The colonel had kept letters from Goering asking why he wasn't allowed a batman in his cell; even suicide notes. There were invitations from the judges to cock-tail parties, Andrus' pencilled record of the actual times of the hangings. It seemed that in eighteen months as Commandant he had thrown nothing away.

Amongst evidence gathered for the tribunal was an ancient letter Hess had written on 16 July 1924, from Landsberg prison, where he and Hitler had been jailed for the failed Munich 'Beer Hall' coup the year before. Hess, acting as Hitler's secretary and already helping him to write *Mein Kampf*, was telling a colleague – Heim – that at the time Hitler was refus-ing to have anything more to do with 'outside matters' like the fighting within the Party.

> I am against any books being sent to him. Hitler wants at this time to have nothing to do with daily questions from the outside. I tried this for the last time this morning, but in vain. Anyway he pulls himself back even more so from the leadership. He will not take the responsibility for what happens on the outside without his knowledge and also, partly, against his will. He is not able to do anything about the eternal fighting that goes on in the Party, at least not from here.
>
> It is vain to deal at this moment with these little matters. On the other hand, he is sure to be soon able, when he receives his freedom again, to push everything into the right direction.
>
> Then he will be very quickly able to finish everything that has led to confusion in his absence about the differences in religion ... he will take all their strength and combine it together for the fight against Communism, the Communism that is more dangerous than ever; because it is under a blanket until the day of attack.
>
> I believe there will soon come the moment that everybody, out of desperation of movement against the Bolshevistic threat will be behind

Hitler … and that is why we hope that he will be let out of here soon enough to regain his freedom of movement.

Even if Communism will not be the cause of re-unification of all our difficulties, the damage because of the fighting in the Volk movement will not be so tragic. The personality of Hitler, with momentous meaning, (I have only here fully realised) will be able to overcome anything.

He will put his stamp on the German people and will put down the cancerous growth among his people. From today on, one does not look at all the in-fighting and stupid things his followers do. One will do it even less when in the Autumn, Hitler's book will appear. That will not only show us a picture of the politician, but also the human being Hitler, shown in the widest understanding of Germany.

I enclose a special pamphlet from Hitler about Germany's renewal.

I spent the next hours sneezing from the dust of twenty years and reading the documents' contents onto a tape-recorder. As we both needed to lose weight, Col. Andrus and I had arranged to swim daily in the university pool and lunch frugally on liquid Chocolate Metrecal, which was supposed to replace food. (I'd spoil it all in the evening at the commissary where I'd pile my plate with flapjacks, ice-cream and marshmallows.)

I spent two more days in the loft feeling I was inside Nuremberg prison; I could almost hear the clanging of steel cell doors and smell the disinfectant. But there was a huge obstacle to using the material Andrus had filed. The printed pages and scrawled notes I was opening in the trunks were historical dynamite. But the most sensational were ominously stamped in stencil: CLASSIFIED. NOT TO BE RELEASED. EYES ONLY. The colonel and I were, if we used material from these files for our book, surely breaking a most sobering law which could land both of us in serious trouble. At any time he was obviously going to say to me, 'I'm sorry. I should have told you. We can't access any of this stuff.' And this time he would not have been joking. (I could see £300 in airfares and two weeks' work going uselessly down the drain.) One file I picked out of the trunk marked SECRET was a note Col. Andrus had dictated on 14 February 1946.

Mr Manlin came in on 13 February to discuss again his firm conviction that Bormann is still alive and that large groups of uncaptured German troops, wealth and equipment are concealed along with him, in the Bavarian mountains, south of Bad Tolz.

He also reported to me that he positively knew that the Bavarian Police had been re-Nazized, the 12 top men being ardent Party members. He said he had reported all this to Third Army Intelligence.

Col. Andrus attached Max Manlin's allegation that:

The last Government plane – leaving Berlin shortly before the surrender – with full crew and passengers, landed at Riem, near Munich, in the evening hours and continuing its flight southwards, destination unknown, was piloted by Capt. Hans Bauer, Hitler's private pilot. It came back empty.

Over coffee on the Monday morning I had to take the plunge.
'Colonel, we have a bit of a problem with our book.'
'Yeah? What sort of a problem?'
'The files I am taking all these episodes from are, well, classified. Many marked "secret". Surely we can't use them?'
His eye focused on me hard. 'Mr Zwar' (he always stuck to formality), 'in your country (he was referring to Britain) things are maybe different. A classification board over there has to sit and classify, or de-classify, sensitive material. In my country, the man on the spot classifies and the man on the spot de-classifies.' His eye was twinkling. 'I de-classified all that stuff this morning.'

I went back to work, head spinning. We either had an incredible book of never-before-revealed secrets, or we'd have a banned book and possibly share Metrecal in a cell.

One question kept nagging me as I went through the Andrus files. How was it possible for Hermann Goering to commit suicide in the world's highest-security prison?

The 'tight ship' Andrus had so efficiently managed, had somehow manifestly failed; and obviously, so had hard-man Colonel Andrus. Goering, hours before his scheduled execution by hanging, had taken poison, defeating the hangman's noose. His act had dismayed the free world and seriously embarrassed his jailers, not least the American Commandant. I knew I'd have to tackle him about that sensitive question.

After our swim I asked Burton Andrus what had happened. How could a prisoner, under such close observation twenty-four hours a day, and searched several times a day, take poison under the noses of his guards? Goering had been searched with the others before every court session and after it, as he changed back from grey Nazi uniform to prison fatigues. Even while he sat all day in the dock, his cell was minutely gone over. How was it possible for him to hide a vial of cyanide? Where had he got it from? How long had he had it?

'For the last twenty years since Goering's death,' I said, 'books have been written claiming that the cyanide capsule had been planted inside his Meerschaum pipe when it was sent out for repair. Or claiming his wife, Emmy, had passed it to him when she had kissed him for the last time. Surely Colonel Andrus, you must have read what Goering himself had written in his suicide note?'

He looked at me sternly, clearly still hurt by the memory – and the question. 'I have no idea,' he said. 'I ran to Goering's cell and was there two minutes after the warder raised the alarm. But by then Goering was dead. The blankets had been dragged back from his huge body and I saw he had on black, silk pyjama trousers. His toes had begun to curl downwards towards the soles of his feet. He had on a pale-coloured pyjama jacket, with blue spots, and one arm hung down from his bunk. One of the guards, or Chaplain Gerecke, who arrived there about the same time as me, handed me a single, folded piece of paper which had been on Goering's bunk blanket.

'It was addressed to me. I did not read it.'

I could hardly believe him. Surely he had? Here was Goering explaining what he had done and how he had done it on the colonel's own 'patch'. And the colonel hadn't read it! But by now I knew this upright character well enough to trust his honesty. He went on, 'I took the paper along the passage to the Quadripartite Commission in charge of the trials office and they began their investigation. I was never told what he had written.'

'Colonel, knowing what was in that note is vital to our book. Can I start writing off to the commission, if it still exists? To the Imperial War Museum Archives … to anybody who might know? Will you sign the letters?' He shrugged. It was okay, if I wanted to take all that trouble. But I wasn't going to get anywhere. 'It was twenty years ago, y'know.'

He went on: 'I was guarding a group of men who could probably be counted as among the worst the Lord has let live on this earth. Men accused of the most horrible crimes mankind has ever witnessed. We had stripped the prisoners naked to search them and their clothing as they arrived at the jail. We found suicide weapons sewn into uniforms and concealed in the heels of their shoes. Razor blades had been fixed with adhesive tape to the soles of men's feet. We took away scissors, razors, blades, nail files, shoelaces and neckties. We seized all hose-supports, suspenders, braces, watches, sharp instruments; steel-shod shoes were removed; long pins carrying ribbons, insignia of rank or decorations were confiscated. We also removed batons, walking-sticks and canes. We did all we could.'

He obviously wanted to go on. 'Just at the crucial time, before the hangings were to take place, I had a mutiny on my hands. One of my officers came to me and said a group of guards who were way past their leave entitlements planned to seize vehicles and drive out of the motor pool and make their way back to the States. With the possibility that there were dangerous people on the outside who would take their chance to spring the Nazi prisoners, this was serious.'

'What did you do?'

His one eye fixed on me. 'I told the officer to take his pistol and stand guard on one of the pillars leading out of the motor pool. I said I would mount the other. I said: 'Let it be known that I will shoot the first guard to drive out and that you will shoot the next.

'Nobody drove out.'

CHAPTER 2

THE NAZIS ARRIVE

itler's colleagues were taken first to an interrogation centre at Mondorf-les-Bains in Luxembourg, while the Nuremberg prison and Palace of Justice were being repaired and made ready for the world's most historic trial.

On 20 May 1945, wearing the sky-blue uniform of the Luftwaffe, Hermann Goering, number two in the Nazi hierarchy, swaggered in. He was brought to Andrus's office, perspiring profusely. With the blubber of high-living wobbling under his jacket he presented a massive figure. He was weighed and the scales measured 264 lb.

'Goering had brought with him sixteen matched, monogrammed suitcases, a red hatbox, and his valet, Robert Kropp,' recalled Andrus. 'I glanced at the Reichsmarschall's fingernails; they were varnished bright red. The doctors later reported that his toenails were painted with the same polish.

'Goering was wringing wet – I thought from nerves. But he soon showed he was rude, bombastic and annoyed. He had arrived from Augsburg believing he was on his way to see Eisenhower. Instead he found himself in a prison among Americans who treated him with cold correctness and discipline. The Reichsmarschall was taken to his room – furious.'

Goering's medical check later showed:

A very obese man about 53 years of age, perspiring profusely, short of breath, but not acutely ill. Pulse 84, full of extra systoles (heart contractions); respiration 28; blood pressure 135/85; weight 120 kilograms. His face is flushed. There is a marked, irregular tremor of both hands and he appears extremely nervous and excited. He is extremely obese, flaccid and generally in poor physical condition.

The soldiers nearby were opening Goering's sixteen suitcases. They discovered a tin of Nescafe and when they probed deeper, felt something hard and metallic. It was a tiny brass container similar to the light bulb that blinks on an old-fashioned telephone switchboard; and inside that, an amber fluid with a fine white precipitate: enough cyanide to bring instant death to a dozen men. There was a second vial discovered sewn into one of the Reichsmarschall's uniforms.

Among bejewelled badges, watches and cigar cases, and 81,268 Reichmarks, there was a case containing 20,000 Paracodin pills. Goering was called back to Andrus's office. He told the Commandant he was in the habit of swallowing forty of these pills a day – twenty in the morning and twenty at night. He had been addicted to morphine and had undergone treatment in Sweden. Paracodin had been prescribed as a less-powerful replacement. By his sixth day in residence Goering's intake of pills began to be reduced; but when his intake was cut back to fourteen pills a day he complained of headaches and sleeplessness. One night, during a severe thunderstorm, the alarm went out that Goering had suffered a heart attack.

'The news even reached London,' said Col. Andrus, 'and I was forced to take Goering across to Mondorf Hospital to have him examined. He was given a thorough medical examination and a cardiograph. It showed he had a fine, healthy heart and I showed him the chart.

'"You see, Goering, there is nothing at all wrong with your heart. Your attacks are nothing but fear."

'This did nothing to temper the Reichsmarschall's pomposity. I was handed a letter he had written to General Eisenhower':

I had received permission (from your HQ) to take along my valet and my adjutant was to follow later. When I entered the Mondorf camp I was subjected to treatment which shook me – as the top-ranking German officer and marshall – deeply.

1. My room is barred-off place with window removed although the weather is rainy and cold. In the room there are: a cot with two blankets but no pillow, a small chair, a wash-basin. There is no electric light, the door has no handle or lock.
2. My valet, 51 years old, was immediately taken from me and put into POW service.
3. Of my toilet articles I have only a sponge, soap, toothbrush (not even a comb). My books, smoking articles, blankets etc were withheld.
4. I felt most grievously the military humiliation because my medals (including those of 1914–18), as well as my marshall's baton, were taken from me.

I shall consciously not mention further details which I can only feel as extremely oppressive. I cannot believe that Your Excellency wished and knows about the humiliating effect this treatment has upon me.

By now Nuremberg prison and the court were ready. On 12 August 1945, Goering and fourteen fellow prisoners were taken in ambulances to waiting C-47 aircraft and flown to a war-shattered Nuremberg to a still-unfinished prison. Goering clambered aboard the plane carrying his red hatbox in one hand and holding up his beltless trousers with the other.

Col. Andrus had that day sent another ambulance to Furth, near Nuremberg, to pick up a thin, puzzled-looking man who had been flown from Madley airfield, near Abergavenny, in England. When the ambulance arrived back at Nuremberg, Rudolf Hess, wearing a grey suit, flying boots and crumpled felt hat, climbed out. After four years and five months he was back in Germany again after flying to Scotland on 10 May 1941, on either a peace mission or a mad personal compulsion. Nobody knew.

Hess was taken to the jail search room where his clothes and his person were gone over thoroughly for suicide weapons. Col. Andrus was walking with Hess and his guard to the interview room when – from the opposite direction – Goering was being escorted. Hess immediately recognised

Goering, stopped, and threw up his arm in the Nazi salute. Goering looked surprised, but did not return the salute.

An angry Col. Andrus told Hess: 'Do not salute like that again! It will not be tolerated. In this prison it is a vulgar gesture.'

Hess, he remembered, stared back at him with deep-set black eyes. 'The Nazi salute is not vulgar.'

Col. Andrus replied: 'I decide the nature of greetings in Nuremberg and whether they constitute vulgarity or not.'

'I took Hess to the interview room and sat down at my desk, with the prisoner remaining standing. He fixed me with a cold, glassy stare. I told the interpreter to outline the prison rules to him. Hess broke in and said: "We don't need an interpreter. I can understand. I speak English."

'"Nevertheless, Hess," I said, "we are going to use an interpreter. One is always used between myself and the prisoners."

'Hess said: "They have just taken away some chocolates from me in the search room. I want them back … I want to keep them. They are poisoned. It is one of the efforts the British made to poison me. I want them for my future defence. By eating abstemiously I have thwarted other British attempts to kill me. But I have contracted some illness. Their treatment has left me with gastric pains."'

'Was he mad?' I interjected. 'The newspapers had given the world the impression that he was and many Allied officers thought so.'

Andrus grunted. 'I looked at Hess's eyes, his cadaverous body and bushy eyebrows. He looked intense; and he certainly was emotional. But from the moment the man in the old coat and flying boots began talking about the chocolate I made up my mind his "madness" was a sham. He was – as I expressed at the time in verbal and written reports – a total fake.

'When the trial of these twenty-four most notorious Nazis began, the press arrived and I had to field questions on what was going on in the cells. What did Hess have to eat last night? What does Goering do in his cell?'

'Rudolf Hess,' they reported, 'showed his disdain (or perceived madness) in the dock by reading a book.' If he changed books millions would hear about it the next day.

Hess was given a letter from his wife, Ilse, written on 4 March 1946.

My very dear Big L. I am trying to make up my mind whether I should go and see the newsreel in which you are to be seen. Everybody says you don't look as frightening as in the newspaper pictures … but elegant!!

Thanks to the ironing done by F., you look as normal and as well-rested as we could wish. The boy WR, who has heard people talk about the possibility of seeing you in the cinema, keeps plaguing me to go. One could of course leave the place before the main film starts, after the newsreel, since the main film is bound to be nothing for children and the American films are so much below the level to which we are used, so that we can well do without seeing it through.

It occurs to me that you do not know that I never received your short, but for you, so genuine, 'farewell letter' that time. Until being firmly convinced that you <u>must</u> have left something behind, I lost my patience and applied to Wolf himself. And lo and behold! Within 24 hours I had it! Although only a copy thereof, the original I never saw. And the brevity and matter-of-fact style of the letter, which at that time of stress for me, seemed typical of you and not to be wondered at, at all, led all the people who stuck their noses into it the wrong idea that we had long been divorced!

Six months later, Ilse believed she was going to see her husband in Nuremberg, only to have him dash her hopes. She wrote to him:

My very, very dear Big Boy,
The day before yesterday we received via Hindelang, your letter of the 31st, and immediately afterwards, that of the 6th of September enclosing a copy of the long letter of the 2nd.

When I heard that permission for a visit had been granted (over the radio) I cabled Seidl [Hess's lawyer] at once to see whether you had given permission for me – since I would only come to Nuremberg <u>with</u> your permission.

Now your letter has anticipated Seidl's answer which will certainly not arrive until the day after tomorrow.

My very dear Big Boy, of course one is like a racehorse which has been trained for years for the start, and which now has this objective taken away at the last moment – but you can rest assured – I do not blame <u>you</u> in the least. I have complete understanding for you and I would have decided in exactly the same way.

Although I have tried so hard hitherto, I would have refused under the present circumstances. For now it is not a question of what one can stand, personally speaking, but a question of personal honour – of German honour.

The majority of people will not understand us, but will draw the absurdist conclusions about personal quarrels; that you do not wish to see me; that I have been allegedly unfaithful to you for the last 30 years; and also that you do not wish to see your son 'who is not your son' – and so on. But since I have been putting up with this kind of treatment since 1941, it can no longer upset me. The only thing I wish for is a remote island to live for the rest of my life with my son, far away from the dirtiness of the present world. And this wish gets stronger and stronger.

Who knows? Maybe this island is a possibility which goes beyond the framework of a mere jest. You will understand that I regret our mutual rejection of a meeting for three reasons, even though it is irrecoverable:

1. In two respects for the sake of the boy – because he is so bitterly disappointed; since he was <u>so very much</u> looking forward to seeing you again which I had so very often told him this was possible; although he was somewhat imagining the meeting as something different from what it would have been: the possibility of discussing various masculine problems which Mummy is of course not competent. I am sorry about this disappointment because the impression he could take with him could not be equalled by any educative methods or explanations however clear they might be.

I know you have a different attitude; you, after all, have not hitherto had to educate the boy and do not know his weak points and his strong points; and where the weak points need overcoming; and where it would be possible to strengthen the many more positive sides of his nature.

2. I regret it for Mother's sake; and

3. I would have regarded it as possible that this violent shock, which would have torn you out of your 5½ years separation from family and home, would have been good for you spiritually. I have known you, after

all, since 1918, and therefore know very well what you have gone through inwardly since 10th May, 1941. (And even further back in the time of preparation when we were all kept in the dark!) A 'family shock' of this kind would have been a pretty effective therapy, better than grape sugar.

Well there you are – you know my standpoint completely.

Ilse Hess said she had heard radio reports of Hess's dock statement, but they were not easy to understand.

Nor why your defence counsel has had you declared mad – but since 1941 there has been so much that we've been unable to understand that one or more things of this kind won't make matters even worse. Perhaps we will get an explanation of everything, one day before we die.

Meanwhile, Hess was reading in his cell. In ten days he had read: *Farmers* (Bavarian tales) by Lena Christ; *Loisl* (novel from Bavaria) by Hans Fritz; *In the Face of All Europe* by Edgar Wallace; *The Bruck Farm* (novel) by Josef Ziermayr; *Youth* (novel) by Ernest Claes; *From Labourer to Astronomer* (biography) by Bruno Buergel; *The Widower* (novel) by Ludwig Thoma; *With a Knapsack to India* (travel) by Kurt Faber; *Heitherethei* (novel) by Otto Ludwig; *A Globetrotter's Last Travels and Adventures* by Kurt Faber; *The Engaged Couple* (novel) by Margaret zur Bentlage; *Refusal to a Prince* (historical) by Conte Corti; and *Goethe and Goethe's Places* by Rudolph Pechel.

He wrote to his mother, discussing Hitler:

The Führer once characterised the difference between the capitalist and the National Socialist system as follows: in the capitalist system, the people are subservient to the economy. In the Nazi system capital is subservient to the economy, and the economy is subservient to the people. Since in existing circumstances, money capital was putting a brake on the economy instead of serving it, the economy was, to a large extent, being prevented from serving the people.

Four days before the tribunal sentenced him to imprisonment for life, Hess wrote to Ilse in response to her disappointment that he had rejected her visit:

Your letter of the 15th gave me great joy, because I know now that you understand not only my attitude regarding the visit, but also you put your own and German honour higher than all personal feelings and wishes. If this sum total of inclinations does not once come to light in the boy, then the whole theory of hereditary is no good. But he always had a pronounced feeling for honour and several other fine, basic qualities which came to light at a very young age and then often remain under the surface for some time, and come to light again very much later.

The heartfelt words of a father to his young son which you sent me recently, were all the more in accordance with my feelings. I wonder how things will look when I am faced with the <u>practical</u> tasks of father VVV [Hess's code for showing amusement] … But I believe that I shall not be a disappointment to him; even if only because father and son will be constantly going on technical expeditions and will be so engrossed by these that educational problems will be forgotten.

Lt. Col. Dr William Dunn, the Nuremberg psychiatrist, was now asked to assess the prisoner's mental state.

Hess had been assessed by his colleagues as an eccentric individual of considerable sensitivity, with a fanatical belief in Hitler and National Socialism. His loyalties and beliefs have been defended since the failure of rejection of his flight to England [sic]; by the amnesia that blocked out the consciousness of pained reality; or by the vague episode of a paranoid nature in which he attempted to find excuses for the obvious criminality of his associates.

His personality is of a type which, under the stress of disillusionment and imprisonment, may show hysterical reaction and even transitory episodes of a psychotic nature.

Hess's mental status is very similar to that following his recovery from amnesia in November, 1945. He has recovered his memory. He [had] expressed delusional ideas which are of a type which may have been present for brief periods in the past. He has some degree of insight into these ideas and – in my opinion – they will again prove transitory.

It is, again, in my opinion that these ideas are not present in such a degree as to warrant this man (to be declared) legally insane.

When Dr Dunn mentioned Hess's flight to Scotland, Hess said he had no recollection of it. 'Then I said to him that it was my understanding that he had made the flight in an effort to end the war. Hess replied: "If that is true, why am I here as a war criminal?"'

Meanwhile, the prison librarian reported that the prisoners were above average in taste, reading a wide selection of books from light German fiction to the classics, with the emphasis on Goethe. Hess was averaging two books a day, as well as newspapers, which he devoured. 'I read the papers from cover to cover,' he said. 'And I take notes in my notebook on what I read.' Schacht was reading Beethoven's letters. Von Ribbentrop was reading Jules Verne. Streicher, whose taste in pornography was well known, had now also turned to Goethe. Jodl concentrated on mountain climbing.

I had unearthed from the trunks a document giving another insight into Hess's 1941 flight from Germany. Dated 30 October 1945, a statement from Dr Erich Isselhorst declared he was once a member of the Nazi Party and headed up the Gestapo in Cologne and Munich. He had been involved in the confiscation and securing of Jewish property in Cologne and the shipment of Jews to the concentration camps of Dachau and Oranienberg.

Isselhorst had interviewed several people in Hess's confidence before he took off for Scotland. 'I interrogated the following persons: Leitgen, his personal secretary; Lutz, in charge of Hess's bodyguards; his female secretary and his chauffeur. The following were their statements:

After having had a long talk with Hitler, Hess concluded that the Führer wanted a negotiated peace with England. Because of his good connections with the Scottish nobility, he believed in the possibility of being able to do something.

His plan was conducted without Hitler's knowledge. In 5–6 weeks Hess was to try three times until his plane made it.

The facts stated above are true and the declaration made by me voluntarily without compulsion. I have signed and executed the same at Oberursel, Germany.

Now, as the trial went on, high up in her artist's eyrie, Laura Knight was sketching the dock scene. She remembered Hermann Goering sitting uncomfortably on a wooden bench – an enraged, embittered man. He had a cold. She jotted down in a notebook: 'His great mouth is stretched across his face. His nostrils pinched. For the first time I saw the ruthless side ...'

The official British war artist was to spend four months watching and painting the trial of the twenty accused of crimes against humanity. Every night she kept a diary of what she had seen and heard. 'In all my life,' said Dame Laura, 'I have seen only two really magnetic people. Pavlova was one. Goering was the other.'

It was winter. In the old Grand Hotel, once the resting-place of Adolf Hitler, Dame Laura had taken up residence. A small, grey-haired woman in a bustling community of Allied judges, lawyers and officials, she was on intimate terms with the men on whose judgement the lives of the accused Nazis hung. At once she was befriended by the highest US and British officials – down to the lowest American 'snow-drop' guard. In air-letters home to her husband, Harold, she recorded her observations. On 7 January 1946 she wrote:

> I have just returned from Lord Justice Lawrence's house where we had a wonderful dinner party. The conversation at the table was of the arts, Picasso. And the trial.
>
> Mr Justice Jackson was there and he spoke of the extraordinarily obedient mind of the German. In the course of the trial he had to ask Schacht – that Sphinx face – an important question. He was answered with an untruth. When he said to Schacht, 'I am surprised that you, a military man, should tell me an untruth', the reply was: 'I will not do it again.' 'Like a child in school,' said Mr Justice Jackson.

Each day, she entered the rich carpeted, panelled courtroom and had to show two passes at the door to the American 'snow-drop' soldiers. The US Army policeman then examined her bag. 'For bombs, I was told.' She went into the court.

> My eye travelled around searching. Then I saw Goering. Just to look at him sitting there you would say he was rather a charming looking person, liked a joke and would show two perfect rows of teeth when he laughed.

He could also go into quick and violent rages. I gathered from a number of US and British officers here that they had a sneaking admiration for him as the one dynamic individual among the whole twenty prisoners.

He looks a really strong character. Hess, who sits next to him, looks as mad as a hatter, and very ill.

He is as thin as a rake and dark green in colour. A contrast to Goering's pink and white complexion; though Goering is no longer fat. His light, blue-grey uniform hangs from his massive shoulders in deep folds. He has much padding left to sit upon and does not fidget much. He only moves to lean forward on the wooden ledge to make a few notes in a small sheaf of papers. Hess also makes notes. He and Goering confer from time to time and then one of them makes notes.

There the prisoners sit in two lines; ten men in each. They are hard, bare benches. First thing in the morning they sit straight and military; then sideways to the right, sideways to the left, then with arms outstretched on the ledge in front, then on the back of the form to ease the pressure on their meagerly-nourished seats. Or from nervous tension. It is hard to tell.

From time to time they finger their lips or scratch the backs of their necks. Poor Funk sits fidgeting, from huddle to huddle, a pathetic and very small lump of humanity, all the muscles of his face sagging with misery. Even his clothes express misery. Hanging black and crumpled in deep folds as he crouches.

There are three whose expressions never change and who are still the Prussian Soldier. With stern, sphinx-like looks; arms folded and tidily straight.

In front of the prisoners sit the barristers in gowns of black. One magnificent purple gown in the centre provides a highlight. The deep rose chair-backs are in velvet and have a sheen.

Sitting up in the box alone all afternoon I had a feeling that if I threw out a handkerchief I could have covered the whole of that force which for so long held the whole world.

I saw the final indignity of those men, once so mighty, now so lowly, all of them standing to attention at one stage as a baby-faced US officer, well-fed and massaged, gave them instructions. They are worn-looking men, many of them bald or grey-haired.

9 January 1946:

I am trying my hardest for a dynamic and powerful build-up of the design, hoping that I can convey the sensation that not only I, but everyone else appears to feel.

I have tried to analyse the sensation by talking to friends I have made. There is pity that a human creature could sink to such baseness. To look at them and study their appearances as I am, for many hours a day, most of them seem to be such as one might enjoy as a companion.

Goering's facial expression never changes. The head-jailer, an American, said he is an ideal prisoner, so tidy, clean and obedient. Funk looks as though he might rub thumb and forefinger together in front of your face and ask for a mark or two.

Goering today was well aware of being 'The Great Man', obviously a thing he never forgets. He is No. 1 prisoner. An exhibitionist no doubt.

One prisoner said he now considers the Nazi attitude to have been a mistake. He walked back to his seat and passed Goering. Goering hissed at him: '*Swinehund! Traitor!*' Goering has now been put on bread and water as a punishment. I asked Sir Norman Birkett how long it would last and he said, 'I'll say for one meal only, or you won't sleep tonight.' But the bread-and-water diet didn't seem to alter Goering's cocksureness and pride the next day at being once more in the limelight.

Again Dame Laura scrutinised Hess, the man who had landed a plane in Scotland, believing he could stop the war. Was he insane?

The more one sees of Hess, the more one is convinced of a mind unhinged. The shape of him even … particularly his back … the droop of his shoulders. Poor soul.

Hess saw me today. I wanted to smile. But his was such a mad, sick stare that I could neither smile nor look away from those incredibly deep-set, coal-black pupils; too big to show any white around them.

I have asked my friends whether it is likely to disturb or distress the prisoners to know that they are being studied in this way. The answer: 'They will be delighted – particularly Goering.'

'Up in that box,' wrote Dame Laura in her bedroom that night, 'I sometimes have the feeling of being alone in a box at the theatre and that the proceedings below are only a play and the prisoners, actors; that they will go back to their dressing-rooms, take off their make-up and topclothes and go home to an evening party. It is difficult to imagine that they will be marched off by the US white-caps to their cells, through that sinister little door behind the dock.

'I often wonder if Hitler, who used to stay in this hotel, slept in my room. I wonder if he had my bed and if he laid his head, uneasy in its ill-fitting crown, upon my down pillow, which is fully a yard square.

'If I get a chance and can do it tomorrow, if I catch a prisoner's eye, I will turn on a smile just to show them I mean no harm, poor things.'

Next day she watched Goering nodding his head in absent emphasis as orders were read out from German documents found since the occupation.

At intervals in the proceedings Funk brings out a little tin box. Yesterday it contained biscuits and today white bread, which vied with the spotless paper in which it was wrapped. But I could see no butter on the bread and I was right above him. Yesterday Goering broke his biscuit in half and shared it with Hess. An American 'snow-drop' poured a glass of water for Von Papen. Funk is in a black suit of very tight linen. His cuffs make a white ring around those soft little hands that never did a turn of work in their lives.

Without exception the prisoners have beautiful, flexible and well-cared for hands; even Funk, if you like a pudgy baby's hands. Looking about the court I see Russian hands that are big and square; English hands thin, bony and red; American hands plumper, softer, whiter and with smaller knuckles than the English; American girls' hands here are as white as lilies with long, slender fingers and deep red varnish.

Outside in the shattered city of Nuremberg the Black Market is flourishing. Cigarettes, like the ones I came with, are not smoked. I am told, but sold for outrageous sums.

This morning I had a long talk with my chambermaid who is about 45. She said of her home and her belongings: '*Alles Kaput ... Alles Kaput.*' And she showed me her poor, thin sweater under her apron with her elbows sticking through the holes and pointed to herself, again saying: '*Alles Kaput, Alles …*'

[…]

There was tension in the court today. A German witness was in the box telling of experiments made on people in a concentration camp. He was either a doctor or a medical attendant. The dock reacted: no fidgeting or restlessness; no crossings of legs nor sighs of fatigue. Every face was turned towards the witness who spoke on and on in a calm, matter-of-fact way.

Goering was not his usual devil-may-care self. He has a cold. There is a red flannel at his neck, a rag over his knees. He <u>does</u> look in a rage. His great mouth is stretched across his face and his nostrils are pinched. At certain moments he raises his lightly-ringed eyes, looking at nothing. As a rule one does not see them, so deep-set are they, and widely spaced. No longer is he the jolly fellow, the playboy. For the first time I saw the ruthless side … He must take eights in hats and his face also is enormous.

I felt pretty ruthless myself to be absorbed in my own doings while such history was being made.

Often Dame Laura, treated as a VIP at Nuremberg, had 'inside' glimpses from top-ranking court and service dignitaries of what was going on behind the scenes.

'I was told today of the examination of Hess before the trial,' she wrote. 'To everything Hess was asked, his reply was: "I do not remember."'

The examiners became depressed at being able to get nothing out of him – still believing him not entirely sane. So they sent for Goering. He greeted Hess in an affectionate manner. Hess was asked: 'Do you know this man?' He replied, 'No.' In a kind and very gentle manner Goering went up to him and said: 'Do you not remember me? The head of Luftwaffe? Your friend, Hermann?' 'No,' said Hess.

All the time, in the most affectionate way, Goering continued, 'Do you not remember coming to me and asking for a plane? And I let you have a Messerschmitt?' Hess shook his head again, 'No.'

Then Hess's old professor was sent for. A most benevolent looking man with white beard and white hairs. In an even kinder and gentler and more affectionate manner than Goering's, the old man questioned Hess about his youth.

He talked of the walks they used to have together in the mountains, the books they had studied, the beautiful places they had seen. He went over the whole history of Hess's life. To every question Hess merely shook his head. No.

Then the professor began reminding Hess of his mother, and a faint glimmering of memory occurred.

From that moment his memory gradually appeared to return. No-one I have spoken to knows whether his memory-loss was a real lapse or a fake. The doctors who examined him declare him to be sane.

[...]

Doenitz was accused this morning of having given the order for 'the anni-hilation of ships <u>and their crews</u>'. He apparently wrote those very words.

Goering glanced up at me. But at once he turned away. He looked ill. Without colour – except at the tip of his nose. He never smiled all day. The courtroom is warm, perhaps the cells are cold. The prisoners go along a concrete passage-way with wire-netting around it like a cage. At very close quarters I watched them file down it today. The snow-drops' jaws girate unceasingly on their gum and they scarcely even glance at their charges.

'Even for a poor mad dog,' she wrote, 'a dog that has to be shot – there is pity in most hearts. A smell of peppermint gum pervades all ... the mad dog is locked in its cage. The snow-drops are cold, bored and so homesick for their Texas, Alberta, California, sunlight and freedom.'

Goering was sad today. All day. It was evident that he had a very bad cold and looked as though he also had a temperature, poor soul. To be a pris-oner and to know without a doubt that he is going to be sentenced <u>and</u> to have a cold, must be a lot to bear. We all felt sorry for him. I admire Sir

Norman Birkett's attitude so much. He is so tolerant and pitying for the poor creatures who know that their days left in this world are few.

All evening at dinner Sir Norman kept returning to this as if it were on his mind. He told me that much as he had been connected with crime all his life he could never get used to the idea, or lose the terrible emotion of condemning a man. It helps one to feel that sensible minds such as theirs are not swayed by prejudice and that true justice, whatever it may be, will be carried out. And if any have a death penalty, it will be because the evidence of murder – of mass murder – is overwhelmingly certain. God bless these rich minds for the pity they have for the poor, mad dog.

When Dame Laura closed the small window that separated her box from the scene down in the courtroom it also closed out its warmth. 'I have bound myself up with my Shetland rug and tied it to me from head to foot with string. I am snug.'

Goering, too, had a rug around his knees and a red, silk muffler at his throat to keep away the cold.

When on 21 January 1946 she was asked to broadcast her Nuremberg impressions to the BBC, Dame Laura said:

If I had an arm three times as long, I could touch the prisoners from the window of the press-box where I work immediately above them. When I can remember to do so I feel a brute to be concentrated on aesthetics while men are on trial for their lives.

My impression of Nuremberg can be summed up in two words: '*Alles Kaput* – All is destroyed.' I am not thinking only of the court. This ancient moated city is a mere rubbish heap. Masonry, a pinkish stone, lies under a tangle of red-rusted girders. Not a building inside the moat remains whole, for this was the heart of the Nazi movement. Here also, the enemy made a stand.

People live in holes excavated under the rubble – black holes. Under the rubble lie thirty thousand dead. Families live in rooms, one side of which is open – a bed, a table – a baby's cot set on the floor above a precipice.

With the thermometer at 30 degrees of frost, people wait in endless queues for bus, tram or windowless train – or bread from a ruined, pock-marked shop. Over high rubble, once a shop, women scramble; lettering on a little board tells that a shop has moved to a new premises – actually a booth, made from old tarpaulins and planking.

When Hitler started his mad career the Grand Hotel refused an agitator. They wouldn't have him. Later he built an annexe where my suite is, for his own use. I often wonder if he too slept soundly on that fine down pillow.

At court, even the unbending prisoners in military uniform have hollows in their cheeks, while others fidget on their hard benches. Goering the organiser, ruthless, on trial for torture and death to millions appears to have a gentler side when he breaks his ration biscuit in half and shares it with Hess – a walking corpse.

One evening she had dined with Colonel Andrus. 'He had impressed on the prisoners that they were still on trial and had not yet been proven guilty by the court. Again there is the level-headed, unprejudiced attitude of all here who wield any power. That great attitude of mind for mercy always overrides the stupid, petty hate that one meets sometimes.'

Then came the battle for her press-box which came close to causing 'an international incident'.

When I arrived at work today my box was filled to overflowing by four large Americans with broadcasting apparatus. 'No, you cannot come in,' they told me. Col. Andrus was sent for and a long parley took place. I was asked if I could go to another box. I replied that I would have to scrap all I had done. The upshot of it all is that I shall probably be interrupted every day for half an hour. I find that the Americans have every right to turn me out. They paid for the box to be put there. Even Eisenhower has been brought into it. The Lord Chief Justice is battling for my cause. The violence is almost enough to cause another war! This has me keyed up like painting gypsies from the old Rolls car – when the first touch everywhere might be the final touch.

She was given four days to finish her picture from the position in which she had been working for months, then asked to take another box.

That night she went with court dignitaries to the Nuremberg Opera House to a performance of *Masked Ball*. 'We sat in Hitler's own box,' she wrote when she got home. 'Mr Justice Lawrence sat in Hitler's own place. We had dinner just before the performance in a little room hung with two chandeliers where Hitler used to give little dos and his guests had refreshments between acts. It is only a step away from his box.'

Next day she watched the unbending Keitel in the dock.

He never lounges or fidgets. He has the courage to show anger in court – and I'm told, below it, when he feels it. At times his brows draw down and his face reddens as I notice. Hess looks like a mad saint. He is not considered insane. He is too logical for that. I am told he had deliberately starved himself for four or five years and that is why he looks so emaciated and ill. He does sly little tricks, they say. Goering, too, is cunning. I hear so much discussed in the VIP room that I hesitate to write things down lest I be telling things that I ought not tell. For in such close association with these very fine US officers I hear them discussing tremendously interesting things; grim as it all is at the time.

Now the Russian prosecution is scheduled to start. The hotel is already filled with bully-beef shaped men and women of an apparently similar consistency, who speak to no-one else; who push past one as though one were not visible; who <u>own</u> the world, it appears. Like square-cut Czars they look, in their grey astrakhan caps, high boots and bearskin coats. You couldn't cut them with a razor they look so tough. Even the American tough-guys look like sylphs beside them.

Tonight I was revelling in the discussion of ancient architecture at dinner and I thought of poor Goering in his cell. I could only get a glimpse of him when the defence started. From where I was, just a grey, drawn face, the red muffler still around his neck and the rug still over his knees. It is amazing how one can be in that court and yet remain so aloof of the doom that hangs over these defenders.

Prisoners today actually laughed – at laboured humour on the part of Kesselring who was in the witness box.

Everyone is agog at the approach of Goering's appearance in the witness box. Is it going to be as a schoolboy who is saying: 'Please sir, it wasn't me …' – the line the defence seems to be taking? It is <u>impossible</u> to feel that these responsible men did not know what was being done.

Mr Justice Jackson has told me he considered that Goering's expounding of the Nazi principle and his own defence of himself was the most brilliant accomplishment he had ever heard. I wonder if the Lord Justice agrees? Later he remarked to me: 'I certainly do agree'.

Mr Justice Jackson made it clear to me that he in no way agreed with these principles expounded. But he said: 'I have never seen anything written about them, or heard them expressed, with such clarity.' There is no doubt of the enormous magnetism and personal power possessed by Goering. He is a tremendously dominating character – perhaps the most powerful character I have ever been with in the same room. Even silent in the dock, one is always aware he is there. One thinks of him even when he is out of sight behind the US MP who stands close over him, hiding him from view. In the witness box he certainly is terrific. A misshapen, gross figure, the head of a bull, a mouth that stretches right across his great face. God gave out no frills in the making of Goering; but he gave him a fascination beyond words. And when he is speaking he lifts his right eyebrow, with the musical note of his voice.

I have seen what the cells are like. They are plain, whitewashed little rooms containing an iron bedstead and as many blankets as the prisoners wish; no pillow. They use their overcoats if they want one. There is a table – too lightly-built to stand on to reach the high-set barred window; and a chair which is removed at night when the lights are put out. They are not kept on all night as rumour had told me. A good library is at their disposal.

There is, of course, no Nazi literature in it. The stairways up to the cells are netted like hen-houses.

Mr Justice Jackson's cross-examination today was not considered as brilliant as Goering's countering, who came off so well that nothing has been talked of except his smartness and cleverness. On Thursday Sir David Maxwell Fyffe matched Goering's brilliance with his own. Even now I hear from unofficial quarters that Goering may get clear of the death penalty.

The Lord Justice himself tells me that the sentence is something he can never get used to giving; and that he always hates it. It fills him with emotion.

At dinner I was told by the man who served the indictment to each prisoner that Keitel was sitting in his cell in carpet-slippers, tunic open, crying. Keitel, the soldier …

Hess looks crazy now. The sickest man one ever saw. Born to burn at any stake for any cause that happens to come along. He has a round, bald patch like a monk's on the top of his head.

He was the first to see me sketching from the box. Our eyes interlocked and didn't seem to be able to break away. I gazed into those enormous black pupils; the eyes of a fanatic, cavernous in that emaciated, grey-white face.

'I look through my window at night,' she wrote finally, 'at the blackish prison outside. I think how long the nights must seem to those men lying in their grey blankets watching the stars through the barred windows.

'And again I think of death. It is there at breakfast. It is there at lunch and at dinner at night. It hangs there like a shroud.

'I can never be the same again …'

Sitting now, in rows in the dock as concentration-camp footage was being shown, Goering shielded his face as brutality and torture scenes came on; Hess glared at the screen and even though he showed sustained interest, made no comment.

Keitel sat nervous and tense, playing with the cord on his headphones and mopping his perspiring brow with his handkerchief. Doenitz only occasionally glanced at the film, but was (Andrus remembered) clearly upset by what he was seeing. He clenched his fists and often covered his eyes with his hands.

As the camera swept over piles of hundreds of bodies Schacht turned his back and refused to look further. Funk broke down and wept. The evidence rolled on with a British officer saying his men had buried 17,000 corpses.

It was – after eighteen months' evidence of guilt – now only a matter of time before the judges delivered their verdicts. Goering made a loud protest of his innocence when he got to his feet for his final speech. He vigorously condemned mass murder and said he could not understand it 'in the least'.

'I should like to state clearly once more before the Tribunal,' he said, 'that I have never decreed the murder of a single individual at any time, and neither did I decree any other atrocities or tolerate them while I had the power and the knowledge to prevent them.'

Hess, hesitant and apparently confused, rambled on meaninglessly and finally had to be stopped by the president.

Then, after the exhaustive hearing, the court rose. The judges had heard the last plea, the final word of evidence. The legal representatives of four nations, deliberating for an outraged world, went off to consider their verdicts.

Back in the prison, Col. Andrus called the defendants together. Standing in the cell-block in a semi-circle, they heard Andrus say: 'It is your duty to yourselves and to posterity and to the German people to face this issue with dignity and manliness. I expect you to go into that courtroom, stand to attention, listen to your sentence and then retire. You may be assured that there are people to assist you and take care of you after you have moved out of sight of the general public.'

'We had a doctor and a nurse in the courtroom and a doctor at the foot of the elevator which carried the men up to the dock,' Andrus later recalled. 'Two soldiers stood by with a stretcher and they had a straightjacket with them in case one of the defendants went berserk.

'"They're ready, sir," someone said.'

First to emerge through the door was Goering. He put on the headphones with fumbling hands and bowed his head to listen. The interpreter's words came to him: 'Defendant Hermann Wilhelm Goering,' the judge was saying, 'in accordance with the counts of the indictment ...' Suddenly Goering's head shot up and he waved his hands. The relay system had broken down and he could not hear the interpreter's voice. A technician stepped across to put it right and the voice began again: '... of the indictment on which you have been found guilty, the International Military Court sentences you to death by hanging.'

Goering swept the headphones off, turned abruptly, and left the room. The door closed behind him and opened again for Rudolf Hess. The words came: 'Sentenced to life imprisonment ...' But Hess didn't seem to hear.

He had to be aroused from apparent deep thought and directed back through the door. To be hanged with Goering: Ribbentrop, Keitel, Kaltenbrunner, Rosenberg, Frank, Frick, Streicher, Sauckel, Jodl and Seyss-Inquart. Borman – in his absence – was also sentenced to be hanged. Funk and Raeder were given life imprisonment; Doenitz ten years; von Neurath fifteen years; von Schirach twenty years; Speer twenty years.

Only Funk broke down and sobbed when he heard his life sentence.

Two tension-filled weeks went by for the condemned men as those who had been acquitted were smuggled out of the jail to avoid the press, and others wrote long appeals to the Allied Control Commission asking for mercy. All their appeals were in vain. Goering made a special request to Andrus to face a firing squad rather than a scaffold. His plea was rejected.

CHAPTER 3

GOERING FROM THE GRAVE

I arrived back in London to work on *The Infamous of Nuremberg* in Burton Andrus's name and found a letter awaiting me from the General Services Administration, National Archives and Records Service, Washington. It was the answer to the one I had sent out on Col. Andrus' grudging behalf to try and discover how Goering had arranged his suicide.

The letter included a photocopy of 'Exhibit AM', from the Report of the Board's Proceedings in the Case of Hermann Goering (Suicide). It copied Goering's unread note to Andrus and a translation was attached.

It had never before been made public:

To the Commandant. I have always had the capsule of poison with me from the time that I became a prisoner. When taken to Mondorf [the interrogation centre] I had three capsules. The first, I left in my clothes so it would be found when a search was made. The second, I placed under the clothes rack on undressing and took it to me again on dressing. I hid this in Mondorf and here in the cell so well, that despite the frequent and thorough searches, it could not be found.

During the court sessions I hid it on my person and in my high riding boots. The third capsule is still in my small suitcase in the round box of skin cream. I could have taken this to me twice in Mondorf if I had needed it. None of those charged with searching is to be blamed, for it was practically impossible to find the capsule. It would have been pure accident.

Dr Gilbert (psychologist) informed me that the Control Board has refused the petition to change the method of execution to shooting.

Hermann Goering.

The Report of Proceedings went on: 'Goering admitted in other notes (found later) that he had secreted the vial of cyanide at times in his anus, at times under the rim of his cell toilet bowl, and at times in his navel. He had switched it from one hiding-place to another and into his boot during the court proceedings without ever being seen. No blame could be attached to any prison official.'

Colonel Andrus remembered Goering's dead eyes staring glassily up at the ceiling, his big mouth gaped open. 'He was already turning green.'

The sentinel had been watching Goering through the peephole, knowing that in hours he would be hanged. He had reported seeing the fat man make his way ponderously to the half-hidden toilet, his arms and legs visible, enjoying the only privacy allowed to him in his waking or sleeping life. Then he lumbered back to his bunk and lay there, his arms resting outside the blankets, conforming to regulations. He had in fact taken something from the toilet pan, or from his anus, accomplishing his last terrible act on earth. In his cheek now nestled a tiny glass bulb vial. At 10.45 p.m., his mouth held shut and his eyes meeting those of the man at the peephole, he *bit* on the glass with a sudden clamp of massive jaws. The potassium cyanide rushed into his mouth. There was a quick convulsion that caused him to loudly gurgle, causing the guard to yell at others along the corridor and burst into the white-painted cell, hurling the door aside.

But the Reichsmarschall was already dead.

In the early hours of 16 October 1946, Col. Andrus, journalists and generals from the major Allied powers made their way to two scaffolds. One by one the condemned Nazis mounted the steps and black cloths were placed over each man's head. Andrus had a pencil in his hand and he documented each prisoner's weight and height; against Hermann Goering's name he had scrawled in pencil: *cadaver delivered*. A German priest recited a short prayer and when he reached the word Amen, the US executioner, 28-year-old military policeman Joseph Malta, pulled down the lever.

Spared death and soon on their way to serve their sentences in the ugly red-bricked Spandau prison, Berlin, were von Schirach, Doenitz, von Neurath, Raeder, Speer, Funk and Hess.

A fortnight after he had been sentenced to life imprisonment, Hess was informed by Andrus that his counsel, Dr Seidl, had made a plea for mercy on his behalf. He wrote – on 13 October 1946 – to Seidl, sacking him:

Dear Herr Doctor,
As the Commandant has just told me, you have brought in a plea for mercy on my behalf addressed to the International Control Council.

I state that this has been done without my knowledge and against my will. I regard the entering of any such plea for mercy as an undignified act. When the time comes I will inform the public in the same sense. I hereby withdraw my mandate from you.

From now on you are not entitled to take any action in my name.
Yours faithfully
Rudolf Hess.

Before I left Tacoma, and the colonel's document-packed trunks, I uncovered one more Confidential intelligence report, written on 3 November 1941 by Major H.D. Boyden, a naval and air attaché, in Havana, Cuba.

A reliable informant on close terms with a Nazi agent reported that the German Legation, in a conference on 1 October, 1941, in discussing the Duke of Windsor, they said: 'He is no enemy of Germany.' When he was in Germany he had contact with Hitler and he is the only person with whom Hitler would confer in any negotiation of peace or armistice when it becomes necessary. Hitler well knows that Edward at present can not work in a matter that would appear to be against his country, and he does not urge it. But when the proper moment arrives he will be the only person capable of directing the destiny of England.

I was working on the final chapter of our book in my Cadogan Gardens flat. When it was almost finished, the colonel flew over to London to check the manuscript and meet the publishers. Inside the walls of Spandau prison, from where six of the other prisoners had been released, Hess remained. Surely his old jailer should be entitled to visit? Since he had landed on his bizarre flight to Scotland on 10 May 1941, Hitler's deputy had still not given an interview; nor said anything of significance to authorities.

Ambitiously I determined there was a remote chance to talk to Hess through Col. Andrus (as far-fetched then as getting into Saddam Hussein's cell in Baghdad before he was hanged). But I had Col. Andrus and his book as an introduction, and could at least use it as an excuse to phone Col. Eugene K. Bird, the American director of Spandau prison.

Sitting at my desk I dialled Spandau prison. Col. Bird soon came to the phone and I explained to him who I had with me. He was ecstatic! He felt sure all three of the other directors – the French, British and Russian – would want to meet the Nuremberg Commandant. And yes – he'd be able to go in and talk to Hess! I put the phone down; Col. Andrus and I laughed and shook hands. This was indeed a huge breakthrough as a final sensational chapter for our book. I phoned Lufthansa and booked a flight to Berlin for my friend.

I awaited news on the afternoon of the flight. None. Next morning I called Spandau and spoke again to Eugene Bird. He was embarrassed. 'There was a problem. All we directors – except the Russian – okayed Andrus getting in to his old prisoner. So, unfortunately, there was a Soviet veto. I had sent a driver to Tempelhof airport to pick up Col. Andrus; when the driver said all we were offering was lunch in the directors' mess, outside the prison walls, Col. Andrus turned on his heel and took a flight back to the US. I think he was a little upset that he could not see prisoner Hess.'

DZ: 'I think he had problems with his wife, actually. She wasn't very well. And he had to get back to Tacoma. I am wondering, Colonel, if it is not too much of an imposition – I write articles as well as books – if I may ask you – on a non-attributable basis – today all the newspapers have published a photograph of Hess in the garden – and as it's his 75th birthday on Saturday – and I was wondering if I could ask you some questions, absolutely on a non-attributable basis, about his life in Spandau?'

Col. Bird: 'Well, he has the life, of course, as a prisoner and it is guided by regulations according to the Four Power Agreement, and nothing has changed much since the beginning of the prison itself. His life is a very decent one. He is taken care of very well. He has exercise and he leads a good life.'

DZ: 'Does he in fact have any companionship at all – except from the guards?'

Col. Bird: 'He is a lone prisoner in Spandau.'

DZ: 'There is no-one to play chess with, or anything like that?'

Col. Bird: 'No. He has, aside from his guard, the warder, the directors, his doctors and chaplain and people who visit him officially. He is a lone prisoner.'

DZ: 'He has never had any of his relatives there?'

Col. Bird: 'No. He's never been visited by his relatives. It is his own desire of course.'

DZ: 'Would he eat the same food as his guards or is a particular meal cooked for him?'

Col. Bird: 'He eats the same meals as the guard – or, if there is something special prescribed for him by his doctor – if in fact he has a bad stomach or something – then he gets that which is prescribed for him.'

DZ: 'How is his stomach these days?'

Col. Bird: 'He is in relatively good health.'

DZ: 'Does he have any psychiatric treatment at all?'

Col. Bird: 'No. It's not necessary because he's in good health.'

DZ: 'Oh, that's fine! I have a list – in fact Col. Andrus, in our book, was able to publish a list of the books he read during the war trials – I was wondering if he is still an avid reader?'

Col. Bird: 'Yes, he reads a lot. A lot of books and papers.'

DZ: 'Would you describe him as cheerful, or withdrawn, or depressed, or what?'

Col. Bird: 'He has never changed over the years.'

DZ: 'He is still fairly withdrawn then?'

Col. Bird: 'Reserved.'

DZ: 'Does he feel – you know, from your conversations with him – that he will ever get out of prison?'

Col. Bird: 'He never talks about that. On this thing – I hope you are not quoting me now – don't quote "the US Director."'

DZ: 'No Sir. It is absolutely non-attributable.'

Col. Bird: 'Absolutely?'

DZ: 'Absolutely. I'll make it impossible to be tracked to you. I understand your position perfectly.'

Col. Bird: 'Otherwise it would be difficult … the flurry that that picture has caused here is … it has caused great upset.'

I had to think quickly. 'Colonel,' I said, 'Col. Andrus's book is a great record of what went on in the Nuremberg prison. But a book by you on your prisoner, Hess, would be sensational.'

'Mr Zwar, I don't think we should discuss things like that …'

'I understand,' I said. His phone was sure to be tapped.

I called him again at home that night and again he said he was disappointed that Col. Andrus had so impetuously caught the flight out of Tempelhof. 'The other directors were all keen to meet him; to hear what it was like caging the Nazis at Nuremberg.'

'Colonel,' I said, 'the book I have written with Col. Andrus's collaboration will be of world interest. But you must know that your own prisoner, Hess, is of great interest to history. Nobody has published a word he has uttered since he flew out of Germany in 1941. You are in a unique position to talk to him, as his jailer. What a book you could write!'

Certainly aware that his phone, like so many others in Berlin, was probably being bugged by his own country and the Soviets, he said stiffly, 'Mr Zwar, what you are saying is highly irregular. I do not wish to continue this conversation on the telephone.' And hung up. It was a risk calling him and I hoped I had not turned him off.

I left it for a week and then I called him again. I said I was coming to Berlin for a long weekend and would he be interested in seeing me? He was brief. 'Yes, I would.'

The next Saturday I flew into the grey, wall-divided city for my meeting with Gene Bird and his German-born wife, Donna. I had no idea then that it was to be the beginning of five gut-wrenching, precarious years: for Colonel Bird, to finally put his trust in me when his most sensitive job was on the line; for me, financially, as I dared not go to a publisher for an advance on royalties. And for relations between the United States and the other three powers – France, Britain and the Soviet Union – if a word of what he was doing got out. The directors' headquarters at Spandau prison was a sensitive meeting place for the West and the Soviets, and any scandal involving the participants would have had serious repercussions.

I found Colonel Bird a nervy, excitable man in his late forties. He was fluent in German; had been retired from the US Army at 41 and then been given the awesome (as he put it) appointment as US director of Spandau in 1964. He was the man in charge of Hess, Baldur von Schirach and Albert Speer every fourth month. In the darkest days of the Cold War he said he had to deal on a daily basis with the Russians who had only one other foothold in the West – the Soviet War Memorial ceremoniously guarded by a handful of its soldiers. Both the Soviets and the Americans knew that the prison was manned by spies from both sides of the Iron Curtain and was crucial as a contact point; a channel for trusted messages when things looked like they were getting out of hand; its directors' mess had emerged as a dedicated Allied listening post during the Berlin blockade, when actual war between the Soviets and the West seemed possible.

Gene, in his colonel's greatcoat, was a frowning, bulky figure with boyish dark hair, a twitchy manner and sudden swings of mood between rather naive confidence, and fear about what we were discussing. He took me that weekend to walk and talk among the tall pines in a forest where we knew we could not be bugged; summing me up, giving little away in case this stranger could not be trusted. We dined that evening at the Berlin Hilton, drinking a lot of wine. Next day we visited a golf course and then he took me to inspect a gruesome dungeon where the Nazis had suspended prisoners from its walls by hooks; the hooks still there as evidence. We talked of my record as a journalist; of the dangers to himself and his wife if any hint of a proposed collaboration ever leaked out. And over and over again he wanted to know, 'Just how thick would the book be?' He told me about his career – 'I finished school in the army at 18 and served as an infantryman in Germany during the war in three major campaigns, including the Battle of the Bulge. I later served in Korea and Japan and came to Berlin in 1961. At 22 I was a guard officer at Spandau – rang the doorbell and was invited in.'

It was back again in Treptower Forest, among the pines, when Bird said he had finally made up his mind about the project: it was too dangerous. 'I've to think of my family and my career. Donna is ill and, as you know, confined to a wheelchair.' His two daughters had their lives ahead of them. He had too much to lose.

Exhausted by the negotiations, of trying to sell myself and my integrity, I was almost relieved to agree with him. Okay, it was hopeless. I asked him to drive me to the airport on the Monday. Now that Col. Bird had delivered his negative decision, the strain was over.

We were on our way down a poplar-lined street when suddenly Bird braked his Mercedes, came to a halt and reached across to me with his hand outstretched. 'I want to do it,' he said. 'You and I have a deal.'

I flew back to my London flat to find a letter waiting for me: a strange plea for the Allies to release Hess from prison. It came from the old Nuremberg jailer, Col. Burton C. Andrus, writing to me on his letterhead of Consulting Professor, Emeritus, at the University of Puget Sound, Tacoma, Washington:

To All It Should Concern –

I propose to work for as wide publicity as possible to gain support for the proposition that Rudolf Hess should now be released from confinement at Spandau and turned over to his family for his remaining years, for the reasons that:

He has already served as long a term as was expected by the Tribunal and as long a term as demanded by justice.

He could no longer be a menace to society either politically or personally.

He was not sentenced to solitary confinement but now, since the release of all the others, is in such a state.

No justice can be served by his further retention. Confinement is for the protection of society and not for revenge, or hatred, or other emotion.

If he is kept on like a medieval prisoner in solitary confinement until he dies, the dignity and unbounding fairness of the International Tribunal will be jeopardised and fuel supplied to those who would destroy the precedent that it has established.

Hess is both aged and in very poor health, reasons enough in themselves for his release. His furthered confinement exposes the four great powers, who are parties to his continued solitary confinement, to dishonour among the nations today and to the contempt of history.

The Soviet government alone opposes his release. Their position is untenable since they have concurred in the release of others prior to conclusion of their sentences of confinement.

Burton C. Andrus.

Also awaiting me was my Australian wife, Delphine. She had told me on the phone that she was as eager for this precarious adventure as I was; I said I wanted to dedicate the next year, maybe more, into a secret book which could be dashed within weeks by the death of Hess or by the discovery of Colonel Bird's secret collaboration; or by the colonel again changing his mind.

The scandal – particularly for the United States – would have been enormous if Bird and I were found out. Sometimes, in the still of the night, doubts would take over. I now had someone else to look after than just myself. Why gamble? Wouldn't it be safer to stay in London in a salaried job on a newspaper, with a real future? Then I would remind myself that 150 years earlier, my German ancestors had sailed out from their village, not far from Berlin, to an unknown land: Australia. They were Wends, a deeply religious ultra-orthodox Lutheran group who gambled their lives on a family decision to leave German persecution. In comparison with what they had done, my hunch was of little consequence.

In the morning mail a letter from Gene Bird arrived.

I feel compelled to write a book about Spandau Prison and especially Hess, as I believe the true story should be told. There has been a great deal of speculation which has grown up about the man himself – the awesome thing of the prison – which will only grow with time – especially after his death if he should die in prison.

I believe the chances are slim indeed that the Russians will ever agree to his release. I believe he is doomed to die in prison. If this is to be the case, then Hess could well go down in history (in some people's minds) as a hero for his cause. That is another reason why I think the true story should be told. Whereas I believe Hess should be released – should not spend his last days in prison.

Then too, there are rumours that he is mad, crazy, tormented, ill-treated. For all these reasons I believe the real story should be told. I am, of course, in a very privileged position to write a factual book on the entire affair as I have had a direct association with Mr Hess since the 1st September, 1964, on a nearly daily basis.

But I don't want to appear to be 'cashing in' on my position. I don't know if it is possible to not appear to be doing just that, and that is one thing that bothered the Hell out of me at the time!

You know, nobody has ever got to really know this person. Hess has never really talked much about the big question and I don't think – as well as I know him – that he is going to share this information with me – or anyone. Do you think, Desmond, after seeing all that and having talked with me, that we can really do justice to this thing?

Since you left I have made an effort to see him more, take long walks with him in the garden, and talk to him as much as I can on different subjects.

I find him an excellent listener! There are signs that he is starting to warm up a bit. I have always had the feeling that Mr Hess likes me and is happy to see me; but he is very suspicious in nature. One doesn't get much beyond a certain point … just yesterday he denied having anything to do with the book *Mein Kampf*, which is ridiculous. He did talk a great deal on the recent elections here, however. He talks openly on a number of subjects. But when it comes to the past he immediately closes up.

I certainly don't want to sound like a defeatist in any way and will put my heart and soul into this project. But these are things to bear in mind.

If it would mean a lot for you to go in and see the Gentleman and look around inside, then we could do the following: come over in December, at which time I would take you inside. This <u>must</u> be kept absolutely secret. I cannot smuggle you inside on any month except for the American month of December, April or August.

Smuggle me inside Spandau prison! How could any reporter worth the name resist that?

Back in his tiny cell, Rudolf Hess was apparently becoming frustrated with his lack of communication with the outside world. On 27 April 1969, reading the daily newspapers, he came across an article in the *Frankfurter Zeitung* that angered him. He wrote to the Spandau directors:

To the Management –
In the *Frankfurter Zeitung* from the 22nd of February, 1969, on page 2, under the title RUDOLF HESS, people are saying I caused a stir in 1941 through my 'escape to England'.

Furthermore it says that since then, there were many unsolicited 'pleas of clemencies' submitted for me.

Because this claim, that I escaped, is hurting my sense of honour and gives the impression that I submitted 'pleas of clemencies' or asked certain people to do that for me, I ask for approval to write to a solicitor, Dr Alfred Seidl, in Munich, to repudiate these claims mentioned in the paper.

I ask for a piece of paper – Rudolf Hess.

In the meantime, Delphine and I were heading the Volkswagen for our wintry drive into Europe, slipping and sliding on the icy roads, laughing and revelling in our new love (we had recently married).

Gene Bird had again written to me before we left:

October 24th 1969: I have been seeing him more often now and have even managed to take a picture of him with his full cooperation. All this leads to better contact with him; trust etc. I have also had a team of people sorting out records in our war crimes archive and have found some interesting documents, written statements etc from and about the Gentleman. I am in a very special position here as literally no door is closed to me.

As we form the book and our ideas up and as time passes, I am sure there are certain people we would want to interview. For example Mrs H., driver, doctor, dentist, secretary, his adjutant (if he is still living). Not to mention Speer, von Schirach and Doenitz.

I have already spoken to Speer and he has asked me to write him any questions I wanted answered. There will be a great deal of work, but so much the better. I also have a complete family history and a very interesting statement written in his handwriting when he was in Landsberg [prison]. Also found proof that members of his staff were arrested; I have not found proof that his wife was, however. I have a room for you – in an old villa in a very quiet area and on the third floor; a large room with a bath. It costs 26DM per night. You could also live with us – the whole family loves you.

I'll also take you inside and we will start the task of putting things together so it is official! The contract we can finalise when you get here.

We have a mutual trust, we know what to expect and the reward is big. Let's make it the finest thing we have ever done!! I am sure I'll hit a low point now and then – then it's up to you to give me a boot!! Of course I must be careful not to embarrass our governments etc. There will probably be the initial cries of protest anyway, but if the book is written right, and it will be, it can be an important historical document.

Col. Bird had said that when he had taken over as American director of the prison, he was introduced to the prisoners by Col. Drake, who he was replacing. Von Schirach, in his brown corduroy prison suit with 'No. 1' on each knee, told Bird:

Thank God you are a Lt. Colonel and not a captain. We have had bad experiences with captains. Today is July 20, the anniversary of the attempt on Hitler's life. Leave it to the army to goof something up. That colonel, Claus von Stauffenberg, performed a cowardly act; what he should have done was smuggle a pistol into the room and held it at Hitler's temple and pulled the trigger. So he would have been killed. But it would have saved 2,000 other peoples' lives who were put to death as a result of this entire conspiracy. I myself could have done it.

I was one of the few people who could come in – like that colonel – into Hitler's headquarters [the 'Wolf's Lair'] without being searched at the door. No. He brought in a satchel of dynamite and it went off and didn't kill Hitler. I was on Hitler's trusted list. I could have taken a pistol in; I could have done it.

That first impression of von Schirach remained with Bird. 'A rather boastful, elderly gentleman who wanted to be heard; who knew everything best. He would always talk down to you. Later on he asked for a monocle (which he didn't get) for his one good eye. He was very proud that he had spent eight years in the US and that he and his wife had had a black 'mammy' as a children's nurse.

When one of his boys indicated he was coming to visit him, von Schirach would discover the route he would take to Berlin and then read books on the towns his son would pass through. 'Ah Bayreuth! Remember the old town square? My friend helped design and rebuild it.' His son would be impressed. 'Oh Paps! All the things you know!' He told his son he knew 10,000 people by name, face and voice. When his son, on a visit, failed to remember someone's name, he scolded him: 'Son, you make a big mistake; you must remember peoples' names. It is a failure on your part if you do not. You must exercise your mind to remember names.'

When Bird first met Rudolf Hess (who he had previously only seen from a distance, as a guard officer), the prisoner was walking – feet splayed out – head down, hands behind his back. Frowning.

Hess stopped, took off his hat and formally bowed. 'His eyes seemed sunken, almost hidden by his thick, bushy eyebrows. He appeared withdrawn, suspicious and mysterious,' recalled Bird.

'Almost daily I asked him how he was and he replied: "Bad! My heart troubles me; my kidneys; my bladder." It was almost difficult to satisfy Hess. He took great pleasure in turning things back. A coat was either too big or too small. He never laughed.'

This was the strange man we would be writing about.

CHAPTER 4

UNDERSTANDING HESS

Berlin was in the depths of bitter winter when we entered Germany to begin working with Gene Bird, almost certainly (he had warned me) under the watchful eyes of Russia's KGB. It would have been an inefficient spy network that took no notice of a British-registered, right-hand-drive car parked daily outside the Spandau American director's residence.

By the time we reached our *gasthof* and settled in, only the stooped Hess was left in the Spandau prison; his two fellow inmates, von Shirach and Speer, had ended their sentences and been released. Hess slept in Cell 23 in the grim high-walled jail, only a few kilometres away from our hotel room in the divided city, and he was said to be a 'loner', refusing to converse with his jailers.

The prison building had been commenced in 1878 and finished in 1881. It was used as a military prison until 1919, and until 1939 as a civil prison. It had 132 single cells, and ten larger rooms in which forty prisoners could be detained. There were five punishment cells. After 1945 there were 600 prisoners serving sentences. Prior to and during the Second World War, 1,200 'political' prisoners were executed at Spandau by guillotine and hanging. The iron bar on which the hangings took place remained. When Spandau prison came under Four Power control the guillotine was removed and the execution chamber became an operating theatre. In December 1954, the current of 4,000 volts in the electric fence was switched on for twenty-four hours a day. Contact with it would be fatal in most circumstances.

We drove out to see it – a red-brick, menacing old structure with a 30 ft wall topped with broken glass and looped with 10 ft of electrified wire.

Christmas was now approaching and it was snowing heavily. We had to dig our VW out of drifts each morning and jump shivering into the car, revving it to operate the heater which was no match for snow-covered Berlin. I had to stop every few kilometres to rub Delphine's feet, which she told me, almost weeping with the pain, were freezing as we drove to Colonel Bird's Fischottersteig home.

He sat beside me on a couch and told me to switch on my recorder, describing Hess's cell.

It's painted dark green and cream, measuring 8 ft 10 in long and 7 ft 5 in wide. It has a black floor and curved ceiling painted white. The lone prisoner sleeps on a simple iron army bed which has a wooden base beneath the mattress, tilted to help his posture. Above his head is a barred window overlooking the tops of trees where birds flutter about in weak sunshine. When he goes out into the garden he sits on a bench and feeds them crumbs.

From where he lay on his bunk, he continued, Hess could see his toilet and the cell door which had a square, iron-meshed peephole through which his guards could keep watch on him. Beside the bed stood a hard, upright wooden chair and a rough-hewn table on which lay his books, medicines and old photographs of his toddler son and his wife, which he had brought from Nuremberg prison. In the cell and the echoing corridors, which rang with the clash of steel, there was a constant smell of disinfectant.

That cell and another, which used to be the chapel, were his home from 18 July 1947; the day Spandau's heavy doors swung open to admit the remnants of the Hitler regime who had escaped the hangman's noose.

When Hess was out in the garden one day, Bird ordered a thorough search of his cell. 'We found more than 100 pills, which he should have been taking, hidden away; little packages of salt and pepper, each one marked;

cheese that had moulded – even potato salad, hidden behind the radiator, in every corner … under a ledge. Tomorrow I'll have a list of what the old man is reading. That should be interesting for you.'

One of the first documents he had discovered, which he believed would throw an interesting light on his prisoner, was a Spandau director's report from six years previously – in August 1963 – when a German doctor had called on the jail's authorities. Dr L. Schmitt had visited (the document stated) and said he wanted to inform the authorities of some facts about Hess which might influence the future treatment of the prisoner.

Col. Drake said: 'Dr Schmitt came to my office and talked steadily for an hour and 10 minutes. The gist of the information he revealed was as follows.

'He was Hess's doctor, prior to 1941. Several times during the Nazi period he (Schmitt) was an inmate of Sachsenhausen concentration camp; he was taken out intermittently to treat Hess and other high-ranking Nazis.

'Today he has a clinic and an office in Munich, calling himself (an expert) in nuclear medicine and yoga; he treats about 200 patients a day. He has been silent all this time about Hess as he felt he was bound by the doctor-patient relationship. He wants to talk now because he feels Hess's sanity may be in the balance. He wants authorities to know that Hess flew to Scotland because of pacifist beliefs, which he had accepted after joining a religious sect, the Anthroposophs, created by Rudolf Steiner.

'Further, he said that Hess had, for several years prior to 1941, been rendered politically ineffective by Bormann and Hitler and that he had been forbidden to see Hitler for two years prior to his flight; and that Hess – because of his extremely introverted personality – will become incurably insane unless he is soon released from his confinement.'

Col. Drake's report went on: 'Dr Schmitt's monologue was startling to the point of fantastic with information on personalities; i.e. that Hitler's grandfather had been a gypsy.'

We had settled in Berlin, and Gene Bird and I arranged to get together at ten the next morning. But he suddenly had an alarm call at home. Hess had been found screaming in pain, clutching his stomach and had to be rushed into the prison hospital for examination. 'They say it's a blockage of the intestines. It could be cancer,' said the worried director when I met him later. 'They've taken him under escort to the British Military Hospital. It's the first time the old man has been out of a prison in twenty-three years.

'He looks pale and haggard. When I saw him he had his knees drawn up to his chin and his hands clasped around them. He was shaking. He refused to talk to anybody but me. When I got to him he grabbed my hand and said: "Will you visit me every day at the hospital? I'm afraid. I have only a few days to live on this earth. I'm at my end now."

'Then he had started to sob. "Why don't they release me? Why must I suffer so? I alone tried to bring about peace in the world and for this I must stay here the longest. It is not right. It is not just."'

Hess had shakily written a note to be sent to his wife and son:

My dear ones … I am on my way to the hospital. They want to try and repair me from the bottom up. Don't worry. As soon as you have read the book from Zackel – please send it to me; the book about the atomic structure. I'm in a hurry. With love as always – Yours RH.

And he dictated a note to warder R. Kyle, which he signed at 9.30 p.m. on 29 November 1969:

Last night the heart of Pr. #7 stopped suddenly beating. In the run of this day happened the same several times; in all cases it has been difficult to get it beating again, that is to say there is a great danger of life for the pr.

I ask the Dr's or Gov's a meeting this evening of the following persons; Br and Ger heart specialists; the lawyer of #7 Seidl; a German notary to make a written statement signed by myself; my Son being at Hamburg Hindelang – he can be reached by telephone (Fr. Pastor knows telephone no.)
Signed Rudolf Hess.

Hess's release from prison and his life sentence, in view of his advanced age and ill-health, had been seriously discussed at the highest Allied levels in the previous two years. Article 29 of the Nuremberg Tribunal was now interpreted to mean that the Four Powers could at any time reduce, or alter, his sentence, but may not increase its severity. Whereas France, Britain and the United States looked towards release, the Soviets were against it. In March

1966, the Allied embassies in Bonn delivered to the Russians a joint letter saying they believed Hess should be released at the same time as Speer and von Schirach. Apart from the humanitarian aspect, there was the additional question of the desirability of retaining a large institution like Spandau for one old and infirm prisoner.

Hess's son, Wolf-Rudiger, had written to the members of the International Military Tribunal that had sentenced his father to life imprisonment, asking if they agreed he had served enough time in prison. Judge Francis Biddle replied on 12 October 1967:

Rudolf Hess was sentenced by the International Military Tribunal in Nürnberg in 1946 to serve a life sentence in Spandau, based on his active participation as third in command of the Hitler government in the conspiracy to wage aggressive war and the active waging of that war. He is the last of the German defendants in prison.

His son, Wolf-Rudiger Hess, has asked me to sign a 'statement' to the effect that he was 'expressly exonerated' on the charge of war crimes and crimes against humanity. It is true that Hess was not found expressly guilty of these charges, but neither he, nor any of the other prisoners, was exonerated. I cannot judge – as the statement suggests – whether he has 'exceeded the measure of personal suffering laid upon him'.

The statement asserts that 'the maintenance of a political prison by four major powers for the single purpose of watching the slow death of an old man is not in keeping with the spirit of this age'.

This seems to me nonsense; and I do not believe that Hess's imprisonment, as the statement concludes, 'is a flagrant defiance of human feelings'.

But both Lord Oaksey, the presiding member of the Tribunal, and I think that Hess has served long enough, and that he should now be released.

Two months later Lord Oaksey wrote to Wolf-Rudiger:

I fully appreciate your feelings about the prolonged imprisonment of your father and I have on several occasions expressed my opinion that he has suffered enough and should now be released.

Now, waiting for the ambulance, Hess's sobbing suddenly stopped. He glanced around to make sure nobody could hear. 'Colonel,' he whispered. 'I want you to do something. *I want you to kidnap me.* You can arrange it. There would be, of course, a scream of protest from the Russians. But once I am free and out of Berlin into the West they could do nothing. It is not a decision they could make at the White House. But *you* could make it. Of course there would be trouble – but not for long. It would soon be forgotten.'

Now the ambulance had arrived and the crew came in to lift Hess on to a stretcher. 'And as I had promised,' Bird said, 'I walked beside him.'

Hess was carried down the twenty-two steps from the jail hospital to the courtyard and, in a light fall of snow, placed in the waiting ambulance. He was wheeled into the British Military Hospital X-ray department where it was found there was an accumulation of gas present under both sides of the diaphragm. He had a duodenal ulcer which the doctors said might have already perforated and closed itself.

CHAPTER 5

COLONEL BIRD — REPORTER

Fate had, in an odd way, come to help our collaboration. Gene Bird could see Hess every night in hospital. Alone. A British soldier, with a sub-machine gun at his feet, sat on the outside of a glass partition, with armed police and dogs patrolling the hospital perimeter outside. What Hess had to say to Bird, if anything, would remain private.

Gene Bird 'the soldier' now had to be Gene Bird 'reporter'; to be my eyes and ears. From the moment he entered the ward each night until he left the hospital he had to note unobtrusively how the prisoner appeared, what he said, his moods, his fears. I would write out six questions which Colonel Bird took in to Hess every night; this was a man who had never said an explanatory word other than his rambling Nuremberg 'statement from the dock', since he flew to Scotland in 1941.

While I sat outside in the colonel's Mercedes, the engine running so it could remain heated, soldiers and police stamped about in the snow, talking into hand-held radios, some of them glancing over at the car now and again, no doubt wondering why a passenger sat in it, engine running, for an hour or more. But nobody approached me.

Bird emerged in his uniform and greatcoat and drove the car around the block. 'Switch on the tape-recorder.' He had, almost overnight, become an expert newsman.

As I walked into his room, Hess lay half-upright in blue-and-white striped pyjamas, a tube running into his left nostril. He saw me and said: 'Good evening, Colonel. There is something to be said for modern medicine after all.' He had for most of his life shunned modern medicine for homeopathic and natural remedies. 'You will be surprised,' he said, 'that this thing [the tube] doesn't hurt at all.

'And let me tell you, Col. Bird, I have just had some brandy! I was given a barium test, after which they gave me brandy to drink to prevent the onset of shock. It is the first alcohol I have had in twenty-eight years!'

With Hess in hospital the prison cells were empty, but Spandau was guarded nevertheless. The three Western powers urged withdrawal of the tower guards who were being filmed for derisory television broadcasts around the world. But the Soviets, whose month in control it was, stubbornly said nothing would change. Their soldiers remained on duty in the ugly towers.

Bird and his senior officers were appalled at what they saw as stupidity and made a decision to confront the Soviet belligerence. 'We were to take over control of the prison from the Soviets on 1 December. But we decided that after we had posted our guards and the Soviets had marched out, we would take our men down from the guard towers and start patrols inside the prison walls and out of sight from passers-by and the world press.

'When they heard of this plan the Soviet director protested: "No! I do not agree with this! Hess may be in hospital, but nothing has changed. We do not have the power here — at our level — of changing the prison regulations; most certainly not the security of the prison." I asked the British and French directors what they thought of my plan and they agreed: they did not want their servicemen in the guard towers. But the Soviet director was adamant. "The guards must stay where they are." I asked him: "Are you speaking for yourself now?" He said yes he was — because he had not had the chance to confer with his government. He said he would do so and I returned to the prison to meet him and be told of the Soviet decision. He did not turn up. He sent word that he had toothache. Television stations in the meantime were showing a lone Russian in a guard tower, guarding an empty prison. The fruitless watch continued.'

It was now early December 1969, in a snowy Berlin.

With Hess so seriously ill, the Russians had surprisingly agreed that his remains should not be buried in the prison grounds, but should be cremated and interred somewhere outside Berlin. 'This was a relief: we had feared that even with Hess dead, Russia, intent on keeping its toehold in West Berlin, would insist on burial in Spandau and the consequent "ceremonial" guarding of the grave by the Soviet Union.'

Hess meanwhile, very much alive, was being pressed to ask for a visit from his wife or son. 'Nein,' he said.

'There was little point in arguing. He stubbornly refused to discuss the matter further. He had pulled his mental blind down on the chink of light that we were struggling to make larger. If he could be persuaded to have normal family visits, it was believed, a lot of normality would return to Hess. But it was always the same. When anyone brought up Hitler, Hess's past or the flight, the shutters would come down. Hess's eyes would take on a pained look and there would be stubborn silence. Colonel Banfield, the British director, looked in on him in hospital and said outright: "Hess, now that you are out of prison wouldn't you like to see your wife and son?"

'"No," came the answer. "So long as those guards are outside, I am still a prisoner." To occupy his mind he had been given a jigsaw puzzle, which he enjoyed. But he turned up his nose at a painting-by-numbers kit. "It's childish. I once dabbled a bit with oil-painting, but found water-colours easier. I'm not a good painter or drawer, I'm more technically minded."

'I went in to see him the same night,' said Bird. 'Drawing up a chair I sat close to his bed and talked to him in a calm, low voice. "Hess, I know what your feelings are about what I am going to ask you, but I want you to consider now what I have to say. I want you to see some member of your family. Now I know this is a very painful thing for you, even just the thought of it. But at this time it could help in many ways. It could help influence world opinion, help influence the Russians. I remember, you know, how Speer had this build-up of anxiety before his family visits. The long, awkward silences after he had asked after their health or their school work …"

'He was listening. His eyes were downcast under the thick eyebrows. "Yes," he said quietly, almost to himself. "Speer used to tell me about it." Then he looked at me directly, his face sad and resigned. "Do you really

think it would be a good idea to ask for my wife? There is still time …
I might just do it. I will have to think about it."

'I left him. There had been enough said. When I returned the following
night Hess was expecting me. He was nervous. But he was determined to
face the problem that had been hanging over him. I drew up a chair beside
his bed.

'"I have been giving serious thought to what you have asked me," Hess
said. "I have, however, one worry that frightens me. It is the Russians – they
are trying to destroy me. I fear that if my son flies in they may try to kidnap
him. They know this would break my spirit. My nerves would snap. I could
not stand it. Colonel, I would go stark raving mad."

'I said: "What do you mean your son would be kidnapped? He could fly
in. He doesn't have to come in by car through the Soviet checkpoint."

'He said: "Oh, something would happen. The plane might have to land in
the GDR [East Germany] and when it lands in an emergency the Russians
will capture my son. I can't afford to take that risk."

'"But," I said, "Frau Speer goes into East Berlin. She goes through the
checkpoint and travels in and out."

'"Oh, you can't compare the Speers with Rudolf Hess. I was deputy to
the Führer. The Russians hate me. They want to destroy me." He was not in
the mood to talk any more about a visit.

'When I went to see him on the following evening, he said that he
wanted me to come closer to his bed so he could speak confidentially. His
face tensed a little. "You asked me about a visit from my wife and son. I have
something to say. But I want it to be kept for the moment between the two
of us. I have brought myself to a decision … I will see them – on Christmas
Day. I want to see my wife and son."

'His lip quivered and tears came into his eyes. He could not talk any more.
He tried again to speak and his voice choked. But he finally got control of
himself and said: "I will see them under the following conditions … For the
first fifteen minutes I want to be alone with them. The Russians will have to
understand that. They will have to understand what a shaking thing it is for
a man who has not seen his family in twenty-eight years to confront them
again. You can have a listening apparatus and even cut a hole in the wall if
you wish, so everything that is said between us can be noted down. But I do

not want to be stared at by anybody when my wife and son come into the room and see me for the first time.

'"I know," he went on, more confident now, "that the regulations mean only a thirty-minute visit from one member of a prisoner's family once a month. But I hope that in view of the fact that I have never had a visit from them before, that they might be allowed to come in together. It all hinges," said Hess, "on the permission to be at first alone with them."

'I stood up and said that if he would make out an official request for a visit I would put his conditions to the other directors when he wished. He lay back in his bed staring out at the night. His thoughts were probably miles away.'

That night Hess took pen and paper and wrote:

December 8th, 1969.
Request to the directors:
I request the visit of my wife and son if possible in the early part of 24 December. It is the first visit for 28 years, so I beg that at the beginning there should be no witnesses in the room. The talk that I will have with my wife could be recorded on a tape-recorder or a hole could be cut into the wall so that anybody could see that I will not put any writing or any-thing like that into the hands of my family. Also I will promise that I will not stretch out my hand to them. My family will promise the same thing.

I beg you to realize that von Schirach and Speer within 20 years had a great number of family visits, but for me it will be the first one. It will lessen the psychological tension with my family very much if I can get this permission. I ask you, realizing it is my first visit, and that it will only last for half an hour, to please let us eat a Christmas dinner together.

It will not matter at all to me if direct witnesses are there at this dinner. I intend to be silent about all these privileges so far as my family are con-cerned. I won't tell them. Rudolf Hess.

'No. 7 had just taken an historic step. None of us would have ever believed he would do it. He was even writing cheerfully about it to his wife asking her "not to be disturbed that my cheeks have not filled out ... and I am sure to look a little drawn".

'He was still in a happy mood when I called to see him. "I have done it," he said. "I have written. You know what the doctors told me today? They said I talked too much! I ask too many questions. So they tell me: 'Leave these questions up to us. Just take the treatment and be quiet.' But I know now what doctors are. I tell them they can't shut my mouth and I will keep on asking questions. 'If you don't want to answer them that's up to you,' I told the doctor! Now that I have made my decision I am feeling so much better."

'"I am still rather tired you know. Through lack of solid diet and exercise. I am still only being drip-fed. I can read for about a quarter of an hour and then I get tired and cannot concentrate any more. I have to stop halfway through any letter I am writing. Tomorrow I start on a diet of protein and the juice of fish, followed by some chicken bouillon, so it will be different then. I am really so terribly happy," he laughed. "I can't tell you how happy I am that I won't be in prison for Christmas. It is the loneliest time of the year. I did not even allow a piece of Christmas tree in my cell because it reminded me of it."

'He was in an unusually talkative mood. "It was my fault that I got so ill in prison. I was crazy not to have agreed to go to hospital long before." He was propped up by three pillows, his cheeks were a good colour and he looked amazingly fit. "I must say I admire the way you have looked after yourself physically with your exercises," I told him.

'"Yes, it is something I have always done. The knee-bends, the arching the back exercises. I do them here," he said. ("You've got to admire the old devil," the British warder had told me as I went in to see him.)

'We hammered out the details of the Hess family visit at our directors' meeting,' said Bird. 'We agreed that like all other visits, it had to be witnessed. It would take place in the warders' anteroom adjacent to his bedroom and a table would be placed between the prisoner and his family. They could go in together and the visit would last thirty minutes. We could not agree to the Hesses having Christmas dinner together.

'Hess smiled anxiously as I walked in to see him,' Gene Bird reported. '"Please pull up a chair and tell me all the news." "Your request for a visit has been accepted, Hess." "Oh thanks to God!" he exclaimed. "And I can see them both at the same time?" I nodded. "But I cannot have dinner with them, can I?" "No. I'm afraid not."

'He lay back on his pillows. He looked weary, but contented. We chatted about the details of travel for his wife from Hindelang, in Bavaria, and his son from Hamburg. Then Hess said: "After you leave tonight, I am going to get up and do some walking in my room and in the corridor. It is good for my blood circulation and my muscles and it helps me sleep." I glanced down at the worn, brown slippers under his bed, the same pair which had been hurriedly brought from his cell as he was carried off to hospital. Their backs had been squashed down by Hess's habit of stepping straight into them without putting them on properly.

'He had one more concern: "I hate tears and undue emotionalism. I have asked my wife not to cry when she comes to see me, and I am certainly going to try to not be emotional either. She has told me she is not going to cry during the visit ... that she will do all her crying before, as a joy to see me."

'I walked into the warders' room and as we talked I saw Hess through the glass partition walking up and down in his blue-and-white check hospital bathrobe, his hands behind his back, head forward, deep in thought. The warders had a touch of Christmas in their room to share with their prisoner – four large Advent candles, four small pine cones and a red ribbon. [Similar decorations were put up in the prison chapel and at one Christmas caused confusion when the chaplain forgot to extinguish a candle when a service ended. British warder Belson, smelling smoke, ignored the strategically placed fire extinguishers and threw buckets of water over the burning decorations, soaking them and himself. Col. Ralph Banfield, the British director, called on senior warder Chisholm for a report. Why hadn't a fire extinguisher been used? "Once you use one of them it's used up," said Chisholm.]'

Now the decision had been made, security and press interest occupied the Spandau directors at their meetings. This would be one of Europe's biggest media events for a decade. The Soviet director announced that he would hold the British, who were in control of the prison that month, responsible for safety. He warned that the Soviet Union wanted the Hesses banned from disclosing anything said at the reunion, and if they failed to do this, it could jeopardise further permission for visits.

British director Ralph Banfield said he had arranged an armed police escort from the aircraft at Tempelhof to the British Military Hospital, and back again to the Hesses' BEA aircraft. Eugene Bird drove out to the airport and briefed the BEA manager. Permission was given for a car to drive on to the tarmac and up to the plane door to collect Frau Hess and Wolf-Rudiger. BEA had taken the decision to ban all media from the airport, but Bird was informed that press reporters and photographers had already booked on to the flight.

The Hesses were informed they could only converse with the prisoner in German and speak of only family matters; no politics. There would be no embraces, no handshakes, no physical contact with Hess. Bird outlined the airport arrangements to the directors' meeting in the absence of the Russian, who had a bad tooth.

On the evening of 21 December, Col. Bird and Hess discussed mental telepathy. Was such a phenomenon a possibility, the director wondered?

'Oh yes. Very much so,' said his prisoner. 'In fact, the Russians are studying this very thing right now. The closer you are to a person, the more you can communicate in this way. Some people have this ability more than others. Hundreds of years ago it was not uncommon for people to communicate in this way; to sense, for example, if one was sick.'

Had it happened to him? asked Gene Bird. 'With your wife, for instance?'

'There have been times,' replied Hess. 'I believe it happens in everybody's life. I have been on the same wavelength that my wife has been on … and I do believe it can take place.

'You know, Colonel,' he went on, 'the more purely and cleanly a person lives, the better he is able to do this. By clean living, I mean no alcohol, no smoking – and eating very little meat. I am actually against eating meat. I can't stand to think of animals being killed for me.'

CHAPTER 6

HESS'S DECISION

When Col. Bird arrived at the hospital on the night of 23 December Hess had the small transistor radio on, listening to classical music. Beside it on the table stood a jug of milk and a jug of orange juice.

'Well, tomorrow will be an historic day for you, Hess.'

'I'm a little nervous about it,' he smiled. 'You can understand that.'

We went over the details. The drive from Tempelhof to the hospital would take about twenty-five minutes. Taking into account the various formalities, it would be about 3 p.m. before they entered the room where he would be waiting.

'"Will there be much Press interest, do you think?" I said it was already building up. (In fact, I had noticed in four British newspapers the kilted guardsman outside was reading, that they had it on the front page.) "This cannot hurt," said Hess. "Not that I need the publicity. But any Press statement whatsoever will help my cause through world opinion." I told him that once the visit was over, he would have built a great bridge between himself and his family. "Yes, I know it," he said.'

As happy as he was that he would see his wife and son, Hess's temper flared when the Russian warder walked into his room and closed the venetian blinds, blocking his view of the outside world; suspecting TV cameras outside were trained on the window. Hess was visibly angry. 'Why are you doing this?' he demanded. 'I'm a 76-year-old deathly-ill man with only several weeks to live on this earth! You Russians even deny me the privilege to see the tops of the trees and to have the sunshine into my room. I can't stand it!' His voice was high and tremulous and he was shouting at the warder.

Gene Bird had a talk with the Russians. A compromise was reached. The aluminium venetians could be opened two-thirds of the way without the chance of the prisoner being photographed. Hess was contented. 'Today I was able to stand a little way back from the window and I could see a beautiful sight; I saw the tops of the trees and the sun was reflecting off the snow. It was something I have not seen in so many years – only the prison walls.'

He had another small quibble. A warder had brought in clippers and cut his hair, which had been growing long. 'But they put some sort of perfume in my hair.'

A team of six men were now guarding Hess's hospital suite – all armed with sub-machine guns. Four of the guards were military personnel and two civilians. A military medical aide was also there twenty-four hours a day.

✱✱✱

Recovering from a heart attack at his home, warder Johannes Boon, an aide who had become close to Hess, had time to remember his past charges. 'Hess was always the most difficult; but also the most interesting. The least difficult? Von Neurath had great distinction and in my opinion should never have been in Spandau. Von Schirach was a proud "I am" person. Always talking about himself. Funk was a joker, always liked to joke and clown.

'Raeder was the soldier type, always the "grand admiral". Doenitz, always friendly; but he and Raeder didn't get on. Doenitz was a submarine commander and Raeder commander of the navy. They often had words. Speer: industrious, hard-working and loyal.

'On the other hand, Hess was a great deal of trouble. I felt at times he took pleasure in causing other people work and frustration. How many times,' said Boon, 'had I administered some medicine to Hess, gone home and at 12 midnight the phone would ring and I would have to rush back because Hess was calling for me? He wanted another type of medicine that had to be administered by myself.

'Sometimes I would be called back to the prison three or four times in the night. I am sure Hess is not insane at all. He thinks differently to other people. Oddly. He has a way of cutting off bad memories. Anything unpleasant to him he cuts off. But anything to do with medicine he talks about intelligently. Von Schirach was the opposite to being withdrawn. He loved to talk about the past … "I was sitting there with Hitler and I told him …"'

Boon was at the jail in November 1959 when Hess appeared to have attempted suicide: 'The French warder – who is still at Spandau – looked into Hess's cell one afternoon and saw him lying motionless on his bed. He was turned towards the wall. The warder saw that Hess was gripping his wrist and there was a handkerchief bandaged around it. It was soaked with blood. Hess had apparently taken off his glasses, broken one of the lenses and used it to make a cut, crosswise, on his wrist.

'When I saw him I didn't believe it was a serious attempt at suicide. If he really wanted to kill himself he could have made the cut lengthwise; he would have known that. When I was called, so was the Russian doctor. They sewed him up without any sort of anaesthetic. Even that wasn't necessary; a couple of clamps would have been sufficient.

'Hess remained perfectly calm. Since then all eye-glasses have been fitted with plastic lenses.'

An urgent meeting of the directors decided to remove all objects from Hess's cell that could be used as the means of suicide: spectacles, pen-nibs and even his dentures. A twenty-four-hour watch would be ordered and the door to his cell was to be kept open at all times. Hess would be fed under medical supervision and was to be warned of punishment if he refused food. Boon was to be always in the cell-block at Hess's meal times. A notebook in which Hess had written his last will and testament was to be destroyed.

When Hess refused to take food, Boon threatened him with a tube for force-feeding. '"Boon, put that thing away," said No. 7. "Let's make an agreement. I'll eat a little bit." He always had a fear of being poisoned. When the food trolley arrived outside his cell, he would take pieces of food set out for the other prisoners, eliminating the chance of his own food containing poison. Often he would mix it all up, or just take the food set out for von Schirach or Speer.'

Boon continued: 'For years he moaned and groaned so loudly, up to three times a day; the other six prisoners complained of this. They took Hess out of his cell and put him in a cell up near the chief warder's room, across from where his old flying suit hangs. Hess complained about the steel door of the warder's room opening and shutting and keeping him awake! Which was the point of the exercise!

'Hess then returned to his cell and there wasn't any moaning and groaning for about two years. When Speer and von Schirach were released he started again. He was told to stop as there was a chance he too would be released – but into a mental institution. He stopped again for another two years. When he complained he could not sleep I would sometimes give him a shot of normal saline, telling him it was sleeping medication; and he would sleep like a baby.

'The thing that strikes you first about Hess are his sunken eyes and bushy eyebrows that protrude out. He is a bony man, a rather striking individual, but weird. He has a small mouth which looks simple. I took on the hair-cutting and shaving and used to use a safety razor until 1955, when I shaved the prisoners with an electric razor. The two hardest to shave were Hess, because of his heavy beard, and Speer, because his hairs grew in different directions.'

Boon spent hundreds of hours accompanying Hess on his prison garden walks, trying to engage him in discussion about his flight, about his wife and son; but Hess refused any personal intrusion. And not once did he ask Boon about his own life or his family. When he thought nobody was watching he took childish delight in tramping through Speer's vegetable garden. Speer hosed him.

✱✱✱

The hospital doctors were also finding Hess difficult. The British doctor – Dr D.D. O'Brien – questioned repeatedly by Hess about his medication and the reason for it, said: 'Just you do what I want you to do and stop questioning me!'

When Hess urinated into a flask he noticed small particles floating on the surface and said he believed it showed he had an infection. The orderly explained it was nothing to be concerned about; it was a result of his medication. 'That's not true,' said Hess. 'I want you to save that and show it to the doctor and I want it to be compared with the next specimen.'

Now, though, he was preoccupied with the arrival of his wife and son – and how he would greet them. He believed he would change from his hospital pyjamas to a suit, and asked Bird if he could have a new pair of trousers to go with his suit jacket. He got up and reached into a closet and brought out an old pair of trousers, patched in front. He stepped into them over his pyjamas and it was obvious they were too short. They needed to be a cuff-length longer. Bird promised to buy a new pair of trousers, size 52.

'I've got something new in my room tonight – did you notice it?' Bird said he hadn't. 'Terrible! Terrible! It brings back memories. Look at the picture over there of the old market square in West Dresden. When I think of what happened to Dresden my heart breaks. It was such a beautiful city and no longer looks like that picture. They must take it away.'

Bird told Hess that his own wife was a child in Dresden when it was carpet-bombed. The whole city was in flames and there was a stench of burning flesh. When Donna had not come home from school her mother feared she was dead. But she had walked home; all transport had been knocked out.

CHAPTER 7

I KISS YOUR HAND

On 24 December – 28 years, 6 months and 25 days since Hess had taken off from Augsburg – a BEA jet landed at Tempelhof, Berlin, bearing the Hesses. Frau Ilse Hess, a greying woman with a determined face, and her son, Wolf-Rudiger, a designer of airports, stepped out into a waiting cream Mercedes-Benz. Escorted by German secret police cars, they swept through the wide, slushy streets of the city, arriving at the hospital's main gate at 2.45 p.m.

Frau Hess, neatly dressed in a fawn, camel-hair coat, with a scarf about her head, stepped out clutching a large and obviously expensive winter bunch of flowers. Her son, 32, a serious-faced young man, in dark overcoat and dark suit with a red tie, joined her. He had been 3½ years old when he had last seen the father now waiting for him on the hospital's second floor.

Bird took them up in the elevator, where he introduced them to the three other directors. The Russian stepped forward, bowed, but did not offer his hand. Nor was a hand offered by the Hesses.

Frau Hess lifted the flowers and said to the Russian director: 'May I give these to my husband?'

'No,' he said. 'You cannot. It is against regulations.'

'But please give him the flowers when I am gone.'

'No,' repeated the Russian, 'we cannot.' The tulips and carnations were left on the directors' table.

Bird took the couple past the guard to a small anteroom where they removed their coats. On the other side of the wall, in the warders' room, waited Rudolf Hess. Frau Hess had taken off her coat and had on a two-piece suit with a white collar and a blouse. Her hair had been freshly set and was swept back with a slight wave. She had on a wrist-watch and, on her other wrist, a plain golden chain. Bird handed them the book of rules for prison visits and they both read it, until Wolf Hess got to Rule 8 which forbade disclosure to the press of details of the visit. 'No,' he said, 'I cannot sign this.' The Soviet director said bluntly: 'If you do not sign there will be no visit.' It was now 3 p.m: Bird asked the Hesses and the interpreters to leave the room while the directors discussed the matter. When they returned he told Wolf Hess: 'If you use your head with regard to the Press and don't hold a Press conference then everything will be all right.'

'How can I say "no comment" to them?' argued Wolf. 'They know where I have been.'

At this point Dr O'Brien entered the room. 'The patient is getting nervous and excited,' he said. After a short deliberation mother and son took the ballpoint pen and signed the book.

'We left the room to go next door,' said Bird, 'and I warned them as we walked: there could be no embrace, no handshakes.

'As we got to the glass-panelled door it was 3.15 p.m. Warder Fowler stepped forward on the other side, unlocked the door and opened it. Hess was sitting at a 4ft square table in his blue-and-white striped pyjamas and red, white and blue dressing-gown; his feet resting on a pillow on his bed steps; his hair freshly combed. His face was excited, aglow with anticipation.

'The moment he saw his wife and son enter the room he shot up from his chair. He saluted, his hand to his brow, palm inwards. "Hello! I kiss your hand, Ilse!" Hurriedly Wolf Hess, smiling but cautious, put his hand on his mother's arm. "Mutti, don't give him your hand."'

Frau Hess stared unbelievingly at the husband she had last seen on 10 May 1941. She said: 'I kiss your hand, Father.' Wolf Hess smiled across the table at his father who was still on his feet. 'We don't dare shake hands, but how are you?'

Hess sat down, as they did, at the opposite side of the table, not taking his eyes off them. 'How was your flight?' he asked happily. 'Did you enjoy it?'

'But Father, your health?'

Hess spoke confidently, brightly. 'I want to make it clear that I am receiving excellent treatment. Absolutely overwhelming treatment and excellent medical care. And I am responding well.'

None of the directors took their eyes off Hess as he went on. There was no sign of emotion. His wife was obviously shaken; but the son, a big, strapping fellow, showed signs of moisture on his cheeks. 'How did it all happen, Papi?' he asked.

'The day just came when I could not swallow, or take any food whatsoever. The pains continued and got worse and that is probably when the ulcer broke open.' He explained about the tests to come in the middle of January which would determine if an operation was necessary. 'I can now eat anything, but I stick mainly to chicken and fish,' he said. 'I have had a three-litre blood transfusion. It came from English soldiers so this makes me half-English now! As a result,' he chuckled, 'I now speak much better English.'

His son, studying Hess's face as he spoke, said: 'Then there is something to modern medicine after all?' – 'Oh I have never completely pushed modern medicine to one side,' said his father, his eyes twinkling under his brow.

Frau Hess changed the subject. 'It is a long time since I have flown – the last time was with you.'

'Yes. Times have changed. And you have changed.'

'And you too!' she smiled. 'You have changed. Your voice is much different now to how I remember it.'

'How do you mean?' asked Hess, puzzled.

'Your voice is deeper, much deeper than before.'

'Oh, you mean it is more manly?' They both laughed.

'Father,' said Wolf Hess. 'This is not just a getting-together meeting. It is a getting-to-know-you meeting. I hardly remember you. I look forward to other visits when we can prepare subjects we wish to talk about.'

Hess gazed across at his big son, four feet away. 'It is such a long time since I saw you last,' he said, slowly. 'You were a little, tiny boy. Now you are a grown man.'

They talked about relatives; about his son's engineering work which had just won him an international prize for airport design. And Hess Jnr promised to bring his father the plans of a house he was building.

There were now only seven minutes left. Then three.

'Hess saw me looking at my watch,' said Gene Bird, 'and got to his feet, straightening his dressing-gown: "I'm afraid it's time. The visit is over."

'His son asked quickly: "Who do you want to see in January?" Hess replied: "It's up to you entirely."

'He bowed to say his goodbyes. Together mother and son stood up and remained looking at him. As Frau Hess finally turned to leave, her son put his arm around her. "Now be brave …"

'They walked out of the room; Frau Hess's head still turned, taking in the last seconds of the sight of her husband. Then the door closed behind them. And only then did Hess slump into his chair. It was 3.49 p.m. He had been with them for 34 minutes.'

Outside, the Hesses were in conference with the medical superintendent, the matron and the directors.

'Tell me,' Frau Hess immediately asked Dr O'Brien. 'Why did he request this visit? Has he got cancer?'

'I do not think he has cancer,' said the doctor. 'I would say it is almost certain that he has not. Everything will depend on his next X-ray.' He drew a sketch of the ulcer, showing where it was and how it had burst.

'I can assure you he is getting the best medical attention the Four Powers can provide.'

As they were about to leave, Frau Hess handed Col. Bird some parcels for her husband. 'They are his Christmas presents.' There was a sandalwood box of Mousson Lavender soap, a pair of pale-blue fine cotton pyjamas and a record of Schubert.

Back in his room when they had gone, Rudolf Hess was lying in bed with a contented smile on his face. 'I'm so happy I have seen them,' he said. 'I'm just sorry that I waited so long. What a big man my son is! Of course he was a complete stranger to me. Like somebody I have never seen before.'

CHAPTER 8

TWENTY YEARS OF PAIN

The next visit was on 20 February 1970, when both Ilse Hess and Hess's elderly sister, Frau Gretl Rauch, arrived at the hospital in a taxi. Frau Rauch had her grey hair combed back in a natural wave over a ruddy complexion. Frau Hess wore no rings but had on a thin gold chain and a watch. She wore a light brown gaberdine outfit and carried a large leather handbag. She spoke excellent English to the director, but preferred German.

Bird offered her a mirror, seeing she was a bit wind-blown. 'No,' she smiled. 'I wouldn't think of it. I'm not a vain person.'

Dr O'Brien was introduced and Frau Hess asked him: 'How is his heart?'

'His heart shows a little bit of weakness,' said the doctor, 'but for a man of his age, is in good shape. He had a perforated ulcer, just below the stomach and it has now healed over. There is no other ulcer that we know of. But he will have to be careful – for the rest of his life – to eat proper foods. Other than that, there are no other difficulties.'

'Do you think the ulcer is something he has had for a long time?' asked Frau Hess.

'I believe so.'

'For how long?'

'Maybe for the last twenty years.'

'Over twenty-eight years ago' (when she last saw her husband), 'whenever he became excited, he often had pains in his stomach. He would come home from the office worried about something and he would have these pains. Do you think he had the ulcer then?'

'It is entirely possible.'

Frau Hess went on: 'You see, my husband is an extreme introvert. He keeps all bothers and cares within himself and that's probably one of the troubles with him; that he doesn't let go; blow off steam, so to speak. What is your opinion of his bladder?'

'We have had the best man in the field examine your husband,' said Dr O'Brien. 'He flew especially over from England to do this and said no operation should be conducted at this time; that your husband is as well off as most people of his age.' (Some months earlier Hess was having difficulty passing urine. It often took as long as five minutes for the stream to commence. But he steadfastly refused a rectorial examination.)

Even at the age of 21, Wolf had been campaigning for his father's release. But when it was suggested that Hess might ask for a pardon, Wolf angrily rejected it. 'I can tell you,' he told the press, 'a pardon would not suit my father. He would refuse a pardon. The Nuremberg court had no legal right to try him or sentence him. Therefore my father does not feel that he has to plead with these people to set him free. Instead, he demands that this wrong be rectified.' He was outraged that the world believed his father to be insane. He said Hess feigned insanity in order to trick the British and to try and discourage them from trying to betray Hitler's secrets. Wolf said what was described as his father's 'insanity' was in fact the outward manifestation of his stomach pains, causing him at times to lie on the floor of his cell, rolling over and over in an effort to alleviate them.

Two weeks after his visit with his mother, Wolf-Rudiger Hess had made yet another impassioned plea in Britain's *Daily Express* for his father to be released from prison. Col. Bird took the paper into Hess's room and allowed him to read it. Spectacles perched on his forehead, Hess said: 'I wish him luck. It is wonderful what he is doing for his father. But I don't think much will come of it.'

Bird asked him: 'What was your first impression of your wife and son?'

Hess laughed. 'My wife, of course, has changed a lot. And now she is 70. My son was a total stranger to me. Although I have seen recent pictures of him, I am convinced that I would not have recognised him had I passed him in the street. It was a peculiar feeling – my own son sitting across from me – the little boy I saw twenty-eight years ago then 3½ years of age. I had always recalled him in my mind as that little boy.'

Hess said he missed his exercise in the prison garden and wondered if he could exercise on the roof area of the hospital. Hurriedly he said: 'I know what you are thinking, Colonel Bird. The possibility of me committing suicide by jumping from the roof to the ground ...'

'Well,' said Bird, 'would you?'

'You don't ever have to worry about that. About that I would give my word of honour, that I will never make an attempt to take my life by jumping. I will sign a statement about that.'

CHAPTER 9

INSIDE HESS'S CELL

With Hess still in hospital, Gene Bird invited me and Delphine to lunch with his family in the directors' mess, a building outside the actual prison.

It was windy and cold as we arrived, and once inside the warm dining room, where the directors usually ate, we began formally toasting each other in schnapps. The luncheon wore on, the wine flowed.

I casually pointed to the high walls outside. 'If I'm going to write a book about what goes on in there, I should really have experience of what it's like inside,' I said to Gene Bird, who had told me several times, despite his promise to 'get me inside one day', that no non-military person, to his knowledge, had ever been inside the prison. There was 'just no way' he could ever get me past the gate.

This afternoon, however, we were both feeling little pain from a lunch of fine vintage wine and cognacs. Bird suddenly stood up and said, 'Grab your coat!' And in seconds we were tramping along a snowy path.

The guard at the first door challenged the colonel and he said briskly, 'This gentleman is an architect. We are discussing the new cell-block plans.' Once allowed inside, our footsteps echoed as we hurried down the corridor. (I couldn't believe this was happening to me. I was inside Spandau prison, the first reporter in history to get in.)

I caught sight of the food trolley, grabbed it and pushed it along to hear what its rubber tyres sounded like as it was trundled down to Hess's cell. The colonel by now had number 23 – Hess's new cell – opened by a sentinel. I made for the bed and lay on it as the old man had done for the past twenty-three years. I was trying to concentrate – through the haze of fine wine – on my extraordinary surroundings, all the time wondering at the lack of compassion involved in keeping this frail, eccentric, but surely harmless old man in such a place. I sat on his toilet and, in his exuberance, Gene Bird flushed it to show me how quiet it was. (My overcoat got soaked.)

I glanced at the rickety table on which stood a roll of pink toilet paper, a jar of Nescafe, a mug and a spoon; beside it an uncomfortable chair. Hess's few books and family photographs were stacked on two shelves. I stretched out on his iron bed with its square rails and a hard hair mattress on which lay a rubber ring to ease the discomfort of his bony hips. Someone had rigged up his timber lectern to hold the book he would be reading.

The cell door was locked by a double mortis lock with a drop catch that made a loud 'clang' when he pressed it to get attention. On the cell ceiling were two light globes – one 40 watts and the other 150 watts, operated by switches from the passageway; one of them was for Hess to read by, the other to inspect him as he slept.

We departed and Col. Bird saluted the sentry, thanking him.

A week or so later, Hess was brought back, in an escorted ambulance, to prison and the double cell, the doctors sure he had been cured of his ulcer. Gene Bird and I began working feverishly in case he died, smuggling tapes and photographs in and out of the century-old prison, often under the noses of the Russians standing guard in the high towers. Hess was happily giving our book-undertaking his co-operation, and as I finished writing each chapter Gene took it in and gave it to him to check. Shrewdly, the old man, realising his cell would be searched in his absence, stuffed the pages in his underpants so he could read them at leisure in the garden while he fed his birds.

When Hess had been informed he would be returned to the jail, he had asked if the chapel could be made into a cell for him. He pointed out that there were two windows in the room through which he could see a tree.

It was cool in summer and it brought back memories of his listening to music there.

In his *gesuch* Hess had pointed out that his old cell had no toilet. 'There are times at night when I have to urinate many times an hour.' Bird said there had been a possibility of leaving his cell door open and placing a flask outside in the passage. But he agreed with Hess that transferring him to the two-cell chapel might be a better idea, with a toilet installed.

'The chapel was cleaned out,' Col. Bird told me, 'the walls were dirty and dusty. It was painted in green, cream and white. It is really two cells with the wall knocked out.

'The question of turning his ashes over to his relatives when he dies was also agreed with.'

CHAPTER 10

TRICKING THE SHRINKS

Today Col. Bird entered Hess's cell for a chat. 'He was happy. He was lying on the same bed he'd had in hospital. He had the hospital night table on his right, with a platform device he could pull across and write his letters on. The chapel organ and large cross had been removed; so had the Durer prints. On his table was a jar of Nescafe, a cup, some writing material, and across his lap lay five newspapers. The chapel windows had been sealed with masking tape around the edges to prevent drafts. On a shelf were two enamel cups, an enamel plate, a spoon, some sugar, salt and pepper. Next to that were two brushes and a comb.

'He had on brown corduroy pants, grey socks with stripes up the ankles; he had cut off the elastic on the top of the socks because he hates any pressure on his body. He had on his black cardigan, and a white-and-blue check shirt. Hanging on a hook on the shelf were his blue-striped hospital pyjamas. There was a 'duck' for urination and the toilet if he needed it.

'He wanted to know: "What was the Press reaction when I was moved from the hospital? What did they say? For me, Colonel, this chapel lives in the past. For many hundreds of hours I listened to Funk playing the organ that used to sit over there. I have sat here listening to classical music with the chaplain." [When the prisoners grew tired of hearing the same records, the pastor's recommendation of replacing them with Beethoven's 2nd, 4th, 5th, 6th and 8th symphonies, and Beethoven's sonatas for piano, was accepted.] Above Hess's head – though the cross had been removed – was an indentation where the paint was a little lighter and the shape of the cross remained.'

Bird had taken some more of my questions into Hess and one – about Ernst Rhoem, former head of the SA, who was murdered by Hitler in 1934 for 'plotting' against him – seemed to disturb him.

'Question 15: It has been reported that Hitler, Goering and yourself sped out of Munich before daybreak one morning to try and find Rhoem. You broke into a hotel where he was sleeping, got him out of bed and took him back to Munich where he was put in prison. Later, Hitler left a pistol on the desk in Rhoem's cell – and you were there with Goering and others; supposedly Rhoem was to take this pistol and shoot himself. But he apparently said: "If I am to die, let Adolf do it." Later it was reported that you went back into the cell and someone shot and killed Rhoem who was stripped to the waist. Were you with him that night?'

Hess – said Bird – was quiet for a moment and seemed uncomfortable; he had listened intently to the question. 'He looked at me and said: "I don't know. I don't know."'

Inside the old Spandau prison were stored the day-to-day records of its prisoners' lives. Col. Bird, now determined to hurry our research in case Hess suddenly died, was hastily copying them. He had access to the minutes of all directors' meetings going back to 1946 when the prisoners were flown to Spandau prison.

One disclosed that on 1 March 1946, psychologist G.M. Gilbert had reported on his examination of all the prisoners at Nuremberg, and he had said of Hess: 'Passive, suggestible, naïve, not very brilliant – in other words a gullible simpleton. Like the typical hysterical personality, he is incapable of facing reality, and avoids frustration by developing a functional disorder – in this case a period of hysterical amnesia. IQ estimated at 120.'

Goering, he said, was 'an egotistical extrovert, who was cunning and cynical.' Ribbentrop was suggestible and passive like Hess. Keitel 'is disgraced by the Trial and feels betrayed by the Führer'. Rosenberg was 'a bigoted philosophic dilletante'; Frank an emotional hypomanic; Frick 'unimaginative and callous – also feels betrayed by Hitler'. Streicher, he found, 'rigid, insensitive ... considers the Bible pornographic literature and has no time for Christ because he was a Jew'. Funk – 'one-time Bavarian gadabout, now hypochondriac and forlorn'.

Schacht, Gilbert said, had a 'brilliant mentality and capable of creative originality'; Kaltenbrunner was 'an emotionally unstable schizoid personality ... now complains he was only a tool of Himmler'. Doenitz: 'A fairly upright character but politically naïve ... has to answer for crimes he says he knew nothing about.' Raeder was an irritable old man with an unimaginative mentality.

Von Schirach was 'a conscious aesthete whose early rise to power went to his romantic head'; Sauckel an unimpressive, naïve realist, whose conventional sense of values was distorted by his blind faith in Hitler as the 'answer to unemployment'. Jodl was 'a rigid impassive militarist'; Speer, he said, was a 'matter-of-fact, straightforward man who recognises Hitler's destructive force and admits a common guilt in supporting him; reconciled to his fate and shows little anxiety'. He found von Neurath 'a bewildered conservative of the von Hindenburg school'; von Papen was senescent, but still an active rationaliser. Seyss–Inquart was 'a cool, stoic intellectual, calmly resigned to his fate'. Fritzsche, said the psychologist, was 'sincere in his patriotism and conventional morality who made the mistake of believing the Nazi leaders and their propaganda line. Now he was depressed and bitter over the "betrayal" of his ideals.'

Hess had been imprisoned at Spandau for almost two years when Dr Maurice Walsh, an eminent United States psychiatrist, was asked by the Four Powers to examine him in depth. Hess was led into the room where prisoners talked through a grille to their visitors.

Around a plain wooden table sat an array of medical officers and interpreters. Colonel F.T. Chamberlin, the American medical representative, sat at the right, on the far side of the table; Dr Walsh sat next to him. Next to Dr Walsh sat the British medical representative; the French medical officer sat next to him. At the end of the table sat the Russian medical officer, with the Russian interpreter next to him. The American interpreter sat near the end of the table opposite Colonel Chamberlin. The French director of the prison stood in the room away from the table with an interpreter, with the Russian director nearby.

Hess took a chair opposite Dr Walsh. 'He was thin,' Dr Walsh reported, 'but his general condition was better than I'd expected.'

Dr Walsh began the interview by asking Hess about his 'general medical symptoms'. ('It was decided to speak directly to the prisoner in German in the beginning of the interview, even though the interviewer's German is not perfect,' said Dr Walsh, 'to establish as much rapport as possible under the circumstances.')

Hess was affable and pleasant during the interview, said Dr Walsh, which lasted two hours. 'He answered most questions promptly.'

Had he taken medicines with him on the flight to Scotland? Hess's thin, bony face, highlighted by thick black eyebrows, considered the question. 'Yes. I took several homeopathic medicines with me.' Why homeopathic medicine? He believed very small doses of homeopathic medicine were effective in maintaining health.

Was he in ill-health before he flew? No. He was in perfect health before the flight to Scotland. Nevertheless, he admitted to the doctor he had taken small doses of homeopathic medicine; along with allopathic and naturopathic medicines, homeopathy enjoyed a great vogue at the time in Germany. 'Homeopathic medicines can be used in either of two ways – to prevent disease or treat it. I used it for the former purpose.'

Had not the great responsibility of being the second person in the Reich caused him nervous stress? 'Except for short periods, important events such as the pending declaration of war, I never felt under pressure.

'Only on these rare periods did I have difficulty in sleeping.'

Q. 'Why did you fly to England?'
A. 'In an attempt to stop the war and save useless destruction of human life.'
Q. 'Was the idea of the flight your own, or was it planned in conjunction with others?'
A. 'It was my own idea. It was not discussed with anyone.'
Q. 'How long did you have the idea before the flight?' Hess shook his head, he could not say.

What was the German Reich's attitude to the flight – had not the government issued a statement to the effect that Hess was of unsound mind when he took off?

Hess thought for a moment as the translators interpreted the question from the English (now being used) which he clearly understood. Yes, he said. From his reading of newspapers while in England he found that this was so. But he regarded this as an attempt by the then German government to explain the fact that they had not been informed of his mission earlier, and to explain its failure.

He had often been informed by the Führer, he said, that any effort to prevent loss of life was justified and that he interpreted this as justifying his flight. He said that if his flight had succeeded in its purpose it would not have been disavowed by those in power in Germany.

Said Dr Walsh: 'The prisoner was asked whether he had hoped to personally negotiate with the English king on the subject of peace. He answered that he had not; but that he had anticipated negotiating with high English government officials.'

Was he depressed or elated when he took off? Hess replied that he had noticed no depression or elation. And he illustrated the extremes with a wavy, horizontal line in the air made with his hand. In England there was some depression. But that was due to the failure of his flight achieving its purpose.

'Was the depression enough to make you cry?' asked Walsh.

'No. It was not,' replied Hess stiffly.

What about his memory, the psychiatrist asked?

'Perfectly normal,' said Hess.

'Have you ever lost your memory of past events?'

'No.' But he admitted feigning loss of memory at times, including at the Nuremberg Trial. Why had he done it? Hess said he considered it expedient for legal reasons connected with his trial. Later – again for legal reasons – he pretended to regain it. His ruse had succeeded in fooling some of the top psychiatrists in the world. At Nuremberg on 7 May 1944, after what doctors referred to as 'constant persuasion', Hess agreed to submit to an intravenous injection of the narcotic Evipan. The doctors told him that under its influence he would remember the past that he had seemingly forgotten. At 2045 hrs, 5.5 cc of sodium Evipan was injected intravenously in the presence of two doctors and a sergeant and corporal of the Royal Army Medical Corps. At 2110 hrs, Dr Dicks (a psychiatrist) enters and stands by Hess's bed. He tells Hess: 'You will now be able to recall all the names and faces of your dear ones. Your memory will return. We are all here to help you.' At 2112 Hess began to groan.

Dr Dicks: 'What's the matter?'
Hess: 'Pains! In my belly. Oh, if only I were well. Bellyache. Water! Water! Thirst!'
Dicks: 'Remember your little son's name?'
Hess: 'I don't know.'
D: 'Do you remember your good friends, Haushofer?'
H: 'No.'
D: 'Willi Messerschmitt?'
H: 'No' (groans). 'Bellyache! Oh God!'
D: '... and all the stirring times with Adolf Hitler in Munich?'
H: 'No.'
D: 'You were with him in the fortress at Landsberg.'
H: 'No.'
D: 'You will recall all the other parts of your past ...'
H: 'Recall all the other parts ...?'
D: 'Recall all the great events of your life.'
H: 'All the great events ...'

Hess was asked, while he was thought to be under the influence of the narcotic:

Q: 'How long were you in England?'
A: 'I have no idea.'
Q: 'How did you get there in the first place?'
A: 'To England? I don't know.'
Q: 'Why did you go to England?'
A: 'I don't know.'
Q: 'Do you remember "Heil Hitler!"'
A: 'No. That must have been a greeting.'

Q: 'Don't you remember ever having used that greeting?'
A: 'No.'
Q: 'Do you know what a *putsch* is?'
A: 'A *putsch*, what is a *putsch*?'
Q: 'That is what I am asking you.'
A: 'No. I don't know.'
Q: 'You mean you have never heard of such a thing?'
A: 'No.'
Q: 'What does it sound like to you?'
A: 'To my mind a *putsch* is an expression for an impact on water, hitting water.'
Q: 'Do you remember a *putsch* in Munich? Did you order a lot of Germans to be shot?'
A: 'I ordered that?'
Q: 'Yes.'
A: 'No, I have no idea.'

At 2215 hrs the doctors had given up. 'At no point did the patient make a spontaneous remark: the sole unprovoked utterances were groans. This was followed by repeated exhortations that here were all his old doctors eager to help him, but he sat up and said: 'Water please, and some food.'

Hess later wrote to his mother boasting that he had fooled the medical experts and was faking unconsciousness.

> I even let them give me injections against loss of memory. After initially resisting, I had no choice in the matter if I was not to strengthen the already long-held suspicion that I was at least exaggerating.
>
> Fortunately I was told in advance that it was not certain that my memory would return in response to the injections. But the worst part of it was that the procedure was attended by anaesthetic in which questions were to be put to me designed to 'reunite' the upper and lower levels of consciousness. On this occasion, that is to say in a state of semi-consciousness or daze, the swindle was bound to come to light. But as I've just said, it was impossible for me in the end to do otherwise than to give my consent. I then managed, by the exercise of all the will at my disposal,

to retain consciousness – although I was given more of the injection than is usually done – but at the same time I simulated unconsciousness.

Of course I answered all the questions by saying 'I don't know' in the intervals between the words.

In a low voice, tonelessly, absentmindedly. VVV [a sign of amusement Hess used in his letters]. I only remembered my name which I breathed out in a whisper in the same manner.

Finally I decided to 'come to', looking surprised as I slowly came back into the world. It was a great piece of play-acting and a complete success, at least so far as the deception was concerned. VVV. Now they believe me implicitly. But it didn't help me. My hope that I was to be sent home in the course of an exchange of prisoners remained merely a dream.

Hess said he decided 'for particular reasons' to finally give up his deception that he had lost his memory.

The doctors at first would not believe it. It was only when I repeated to them all the questions that they had put to me during my 'unconscious' state, and when I repeated the play-acting of my 'coming to' and put on the whole mode of speech and tone which I used at that time, it was only then that they had admitted how I had pulled their legs.

Prison censors showed Hess's letter to psychiatrist Dr Dicks, but he refused to believe Hess had been faking amnesia. He wrote in his report:

The patient has made a dramatic recovery from the temporary affection of his memory, which now functions very fully and accurately. I cannot accept his own statement that the memory loss never existed. There was, at the time, a true partial dissociation of the personality, which permitted the patient to 'take in' what was going on around him but caused difficulty of recall.

It is a case of preferring to have duped us, to having shown temporary weakness.

Hess was particularly derogatory in his assessment of British psychiatrist Dr J.R. Rees, who had thirty-five sessions with Hess over a total of sixty hours:

> He had funny eyes when he visited me for the first time. He also used to speak of a case of autosuggestion which I had become a victim of. His case was particularly grotesque because he was a psychiatrist of great fame. He had no idea that he should have been his own patient and when I told him so, he didn't believe it and considered it a bad joke.

Now, at the end of the two-hour interrogation with the American psychiatrist, Dr Walsh, Hess asked if he might make a statement. Dr Walsh recalled:

> With considerable dignity and with great emphasis he stated, in a very formal manner, that he regarded his present imprisonment as dishonourable and unjust. He said that at times he and his comrades were insufficiently fed and made to do hard labour, which was contrary to the sentence of the Nuremberg Tribunal. He requested that he should be given his liberty.

When the session was over, Dr Walsh went away to write his report which he published in *The Archives of General Psychiatry*.

Hess, he wrote, had made great efforts to impress him with his sincerity and normality. 'He was most courteous and responsive, looking directly into the eyes of the interviewer while speaking. He did not give the impression of being grandiose or of over-estimating his own importance; but rather, an impression of some humility, considerable quiet reassurance, was gained.' The psychiatrist summed up Hess as 'an individual of superior intelligence with schizoid personality traits'. He also admitted to having been 'seduced by his narcissism'. He added: 'It is precisely this seductive attraction which gained an audience for narcissistic leaders such as Hitler.'

Years later, the doctor revealed that his report of the Hess interrogation had been censored. 'It was thus a matter of concern for me,' he wrote in the publication *General Psychiatry*, 'when the Surgeon of the Berlin garrison informed me that I should omit any reference to mental disease from my report of Hess, stating that the political situation between the United States

Government and the Russian Government was tense – *and that war could break out at any moment.*'

With tension between the West and the Soviets easing, Dr Walsh was more confident to go public with his long-held concerns. In an interview with a Los Angeles newspaper he revealed that not only was he banned from talking about Hess's psychotic state of mind, but a British colleague, Dr J.R. Rees, who had examined Hess in England after his flight, had been censored as well!

In October 1967 I contacted Dr Walsh. He told me he thought Dr Rees was still practising in London. If what Dr Walsh was claiming was true, it meant Churchill himself *had connived* in a falsification; a cover-up which would have changed the course of history.

Dr J.R. Rees had been a member of the psychiatric team that first examined Hess soon after his arrival. Feeling there wasn't much chance of finding him still practising, I opened the L–Z London phone directory. There was a Dr Rees listed, with rooms just off Baker Street. I phoned and checked it was the same man. It was, and his receptionist made me an appointment.

I took a taxi to the former brigadier's rooms. Here was the man who all those years before had questioned Rudolf Hess day after day! It was a warm summer's day and the doctor asked me into his surgery, puffing on a cigarette and wearing shirtsleeves; a small, intense man with (as Hess said) arresting eyes.

I showed him the typescript of what his colleague Dr Walsh had said in his historic statement. Dr Rees read it. 'Not only was Dr Walsh forced to "fudge" his findings. So was I!' he said. Dr Rees explained that he had been a consultant psychiatrist with the British Army and had seen Hess two weeks after he parachuted into Scotland. 'He had been under the care of Dr Gibson Graham, physician in charge of Drymen Hospital, which was near where he landed. I was asked to go to Mytchett Court at Aldershot, an old house the Army had taken over. Hess and I were alone together. I had no German but he had adequate English. I was with him, for the first time, for about an hour and a half.

'After this examination, followed by others, I made it known that I was going to put out my report to the Army Medical Service that Hess was mentally ill. I was going to report:

In my opinion Hess is a man of unstable mentality and has almost certainly been like that since adolescence. In technical language I should, on my present acquaintanceship, diagnose him as a psychopathic personality of the schizophrenic type, i.e. a tendency to a splitting of his personality. He is – as many of these people are – suggestible and liable to hysterical symptom formation. Because of his constitutional make-up and the kind of life he has led of recent years, he is at present in some danger of a more marked depressive reaction now that he feels frustrated.

'However,' Dr Rees told me, 'just before I was to make my official report, the Prime Minister, Winston Churchill, passed word down that "we would not refer to Hess's mental illness, but stress other aspects of the matter". Churchill made it known that he wanted me to stress Hess's amnesia and the fact that he was "open to suggestion and quaint ideas". *Churchill was ordering me to fake my report.* But there <u>was</u> schizophrenia. It was real enough. And if anybody was schizophrenic they could have been repatriable under the rules of war. If Hess was termed insane he would have had to be sent back to Germany. That wasn't good politics. He would have gone back a hero. If I had sent my report in saying he was schizophrenic he would have been put in a mental asylum.

'I did not feel it was a good plan, medically speaking, and certainly not politically speaking. There was also a technical problem with Hess's prisoner status; it had not been decided whether he was a prisoner of war or a prisoner of State. So I took out the word "schizophrenic". I only referred to his personality as being "psychopathic". Churchill hoped Hess might know a lot more about Hitler's plans than he had revealed. They had intelligence fellows with him all the time trying to find out. Bits of Hess's condition were an act; there was an hysterical element in it. But his amnesia was hysterical and quite genuine. We predicted that he would recover from this amnesia when he got to court, which in fact he did.'

Dr Rees went on to say that he was deeply concerned that the release from Spandau of Albert Speer and Baldur von Schirach would leave Rudolf Hess in solitary confinement. 'It will have a frightful effect on his mind. For any unstable man to be in solitary confinement is wrong by every known principle.'

I went back to my flat and transcribed the extraordinary interview from the tape I had made, then crossed the road to Sloane Square Post Office and posted it to Dr Rees for checking. I asked him to initial any alteration he wished to make and to sign each page as being a true and correct version of what he had told me. He was 77 years old and it was many years since he had examined Hess. Would he perhaps have second thoughts when he read the transcript?

Nothing happened for two weeks and I suspected the worst. He had obviously got cold feet. I made a phone call to his elderly receptionist. Had Dr Rees received my letter? He came to the phone. 'I am seriously disturbed by what you have written,' he said.

'But Dr Rees! What I sent you is a verbatim record of what you said!' Was he going to pull the carpet away?

'Oh,' he replied. 'That part is alright. It's just that you have me smoking and in shirtsleeves. I don't want people to think I attend my patients like that. Seeing you was different than seeing a patient; I hope you make that clear. The rest is true. It is what happened. I have signed it and will send it back to you. But please do not give the impression that this is how I generally greet my patients.'

And Hess himself had wanted publication of Dr Rees's findings. He wrote from his Nuremberg cell, two days before the judges announced their verdict, to Rees in London, heading his letter: 'Rudolf Hess, Nuremberg, Prison of the So-called War Criminals'.

Dear Dr Rees,
Dr Gilbert informed me of your wish to get a confirmation from me that I would like to see that the doctors who took care of me in England and later in Nuremberg, publish their reports and medical records concerning me, for scientific purposes.

Therefore I would like to inform you that I would welcome such publication very much, however, not because I think that the public will be better informed afterwards, as Dr Gilbert said; instead, I would welcome the publication because it can be looked upon as an additional proof for the fact that in a manner still unknown, people are put into a state similar to the one that can be reached through hypnosis (posthypnotic suggestion) – a state in which the will of those persons that were put into it is shut out and in which they do anything that is suggested into them, without them knowing what is happening to them.

In the case before us, proof has been established that even honourable men – physicians and experts of high esteem – were forced by this suggestive behaviour to commit the most horrible crimes and at the same time, to pass judgement in a way that would contradict the truth so that the crimes could be covered up.

The only condition for the permission to publish the said records is that this letter will be published fully with it.

Respectfully,

(Signed) Rudolf Hess.

In a P.S. Dr Gilbert stated:

I hereby confirm that I received the original of the above letter in order to pass it on to Dr Rees.

Dr G.M. Gilbert. Sept 28 [19]46.

CHAPTER 11

PUNISH HIM!

Back in Berlin in 1969, Colonel Bird was spending secret hours at the prison going through the fading written records of the directors' meetings and removing them to be read by me onto tape.

January 9, 1948: Hess asked the Governors for permission to lie down in his bed in his cell before 5pm if he had pains in his stomach; and not to have to work. The decision was to allow the prisoner to sit down on his bed, but not lie down before 5pm, except on holidays.

February 6, 1948: The Governors could not come to a decision on the matter of disciplinary action on Hess [no mention of his misdemeanour]. The Russian Governor requested that the matter be referred to the Legal Committee. Hess to be informed at a later date of any further punishment.

February 25, 1948: The Physician proposed that Hess receive an additional blanket and a hot water bottle. This was allowed.

March 17, 1948: Hess was summoned for an interview where it was agreed to lower his punishment term from 14 days to 10 days if he gives his word not to violate the prison procedure in future. He gave no firm promise.

There was again no mention of the actual reason for his punishment. But there were always domestic disputes between the Nazi prisoners and their jailers – particularly regarding mail and food. When Hess complained about his failure to receive letters from his wife, the chief censor countered by pointing out that Hess's and Baldur von Schirach's mail had been intercepted and some packages disposed of. Von Schirach had been sent a package containing a pipe and a bar of soap. The pipe had been placed in the prisoner's personal property to be handed over when needed. Another parcel of sugar, sardines and an Easter greeting card was returned to the sender, though von Schirach was allowed to have the card. Hess had been sent three books and these had been placed in the prison library.

Then Bird made a dramatic discovery involving Nuremberg and Hess's cell activity during the tribunal hearings. He and I had been stepping over an old cardboard carton in Bird's garage as we got together each evening to go through the old directors' files. On this occasion Gene picked up the carton and carried it into the house where he opened it up. It contained thick manila folders and many pages of foolscap covered in spidery writing. 'The Nuremberg librarian passed this on to us at Spandau,' he said. 'I have no idea what's in it.'

Donna, Gene's German-born wife, started reading. 'Gene!' she almost shouted. 'These are all Rudolf Hess's writings! They are in his hand, and all the typewritten pages have been typed on a capitals machine. They are his as well.'

She immediately began translating: 'He says he believed he would one day leave Nuremberg as a free man and that with the full co-operation of the Allies he was to become "the new Führer of Germany"!'

Hess's sixty-eight-page 'address to the nation', which nobody had ever bothered to read until now, began first with bulletins that would be published in the press under his direction. There were specific directives about labour, about food distribution, about liaison with Germany's occupying powers. His tailor was to make a new uniform for the leader, with flared breeches and adjustable seams, 'because', wrote Hess, 'I will probably put on weight when I am released'.

'I have,' Hess announced in Bulletin One, 'with the agreement of the Western Occupation Forces, taken over the leadership of the German Government in the area of the Western Zones of Germany.'

I have, therewith, taken over the leadership of the destiny of the German people in a situation which could not be imagined to be more desperate.

I feel it, and I know everybody feels it.

Even so, a salvation is possible, every bit as possible as it was after the seizure of power in 1933; even though the situation today is far more serious.

But even at that time millions had given up hope. Was it not true that a dozen governments had failed because of the difficulties? With every government, Germany went further and further downwards. The decline seemed impossible to stop. In spite of the lack of courage and the predictions of the experts, the decline was arrested and it changed to a constant ascension. The change of the fate of our people would have been final if the war had not come.

Germany's people will not be saved by fighting against one another or by pushing the responsibility one to another, or worrying about things which cannot be changed any more.

In doing this, they only avert themselves from the problems that they have to solve. The provisions for salvation are that from all sides there will be a line drawn under everything that is past, and that men of goodwill will find themselves coming together to help solve the terrible need of the people and start again rebuilding everything from the beginning. In this sense I appeal to the whole German people. To exclude, from the very beginning, the great mistake, I turn to the mass of my Nationalistic Party members. As understandable as it would be, I do not want them to take any sort of revenge on those who have charged us with slander or backbiting. My wish is that everybody sees in the former opponent a member now of the same big folk community, with the same fate, with the same needs, and the same duty. That duty is to concentrate together, on great aims.

Everyone should keep in mind that there are elements among us who have an interest in all kinds of clashes with the occupation forces. Everybody must be aware that there is an influence present on both sides which sets people into an abnormal mental condition and can force them to deeds which they would normally never have been able to commit.

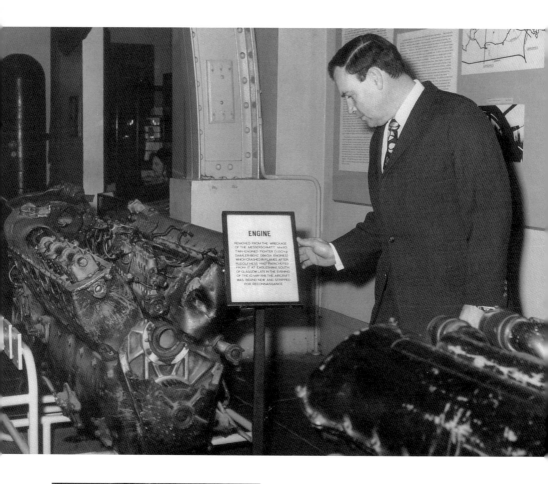

1. Col. Eugene K. Bird with the engine of Hess's Messerschmitt. (*Col. E.K. Bird*)

2. Col. Eugene K. Bird. (*Col. E.K. Bird*)

6850th INTERNAL SECURITY DETACHMENT
INTERNATIONAL MILITARY TRIBUNAL
NURNBERG, GERMANY
APO 124-A, U. S. ARMY

Weights and heights of the condemmed men:

NAME	WEIGHT (lbs)		Height (In.)
Goering, Herman	192		5:10
von Ribbentrop, Joachim	159	1:11	6:1
Keitel, Wilhelm	177	1:18	6:½
Kaltenbrunner, Ernst	172	1:36	6:4
Rosenberg, Alfred	165	1:42	5:11
Frank, Hans	172	1:57	5:10
Frick, Wilhelm	158	2:06	5:10
Streicher, Juluis	160	2:13	5:4
Sauckel, Fritz	158	2:25	5:7
Jodl, Alfred	153	2:33	5:9
Seyss-Inquart, Artur	164	2:45	5:11

3. Details of the hangings. (*Author's collection*)

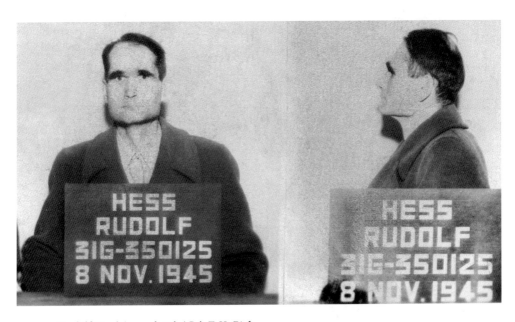

4. Rudolf Hess's 'mug shots'. (*Col. E.K. Bird*)

5. Hess's flying suit. (*Col. E.K. Bird*)

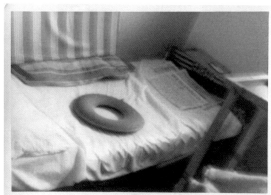

6. Hess's cell. On top of his bed is a rubber ring used for seating comfort. He sleeps with a board under his mattress. (*Col. E.K. Bird*)

7. Hess's aeroplane after the crash. (*Col. E.K. Bird*)

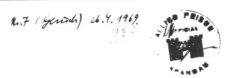

Nr.7 (Gesuch) 26.4.1969

ALLIED PRISON OFFICIAL SPANDAU

An die Direktion

In der ›Frankfurter Zeitung‹ vom 22.IV.69 ist auf S.2 unter der Überschrift ›Rudolf Heß‹ die Rede davon, ich hätte 1941 durch meine ›Flucht nach England‹ Aufsehen erregt. Weiter heißt er, inzwischen seien ›viele Gnadengesuche‹ für mich eingereicht worden.

Da die Behauptung, ich sei geflüchtet, meine Ehre verletzt und der Eindruck entstehen kann, ich hätte Gnadengesuche eingereicht oder jemanden beauftragt solche einzureichen, bitte ich zu genehmigen, daß ich meinen Rechtsanwalt Dr. Alfred Seidl, München, schreibe, er möge eine Berichtigung verlangen.

Ich bitte hierzu um einen Bogen Papier.

Rudolf Heß.

27.IV.69.

8. Hess's *gesuch* (request). (Col. E.K. Bird)

9. Hess's library. (Col. E.K. Bird)

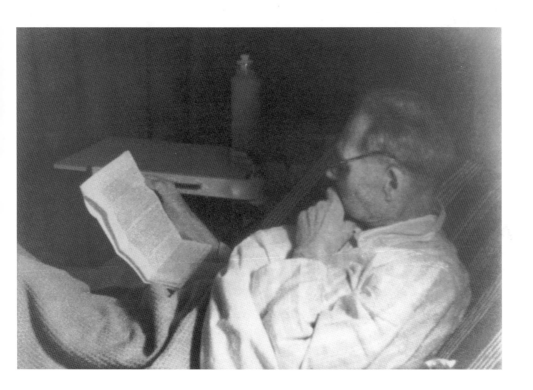

10. Hess reading my chapter. (Col. E.K. Bird)

11. Hess's answers to some of the author's questions. (Author's collection)

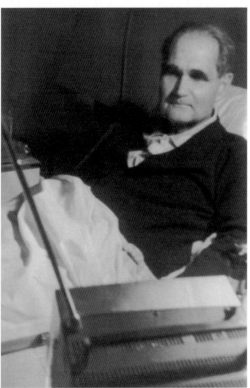

12. Hess examines his flying suit. (*Col. E.K. Bird*)

13. Hess watching television for the first time. (*Col. E.K. Bird*)

14. Hess reading a chapter. (*Col. E.K. Bird*)

15. Hess's corrections. (*Col. E.K. Bird*)

16. Hess's letter, written on his way to hospital. (*Col. E.K. Bird*)

17. Von Schirach's request for Hess on a toilet-paper wrapper. (*Col. E.K. Bird*)

I call on those who still have enough strength of mind and control over themselves to make it their duty to see that peace and discipline is practised. In the case of provocations they will have to show the provocateurs that they know they are talking with people who are not in their right mind. If the trouble-makers are foreigners, call immediately on the foreign occupation forces and ask them to take steps immediately. Relationships with the occupation forces and their governments must be fully correct. Their orders must be carried out and the German people will be quiet and dignified. The sooner they do this the sooner they will receive help in their hour of need - and the sooner we shall gain a lasting peace for our people.

Meticulously, Rudolf Hess had drawn up a list of people he wanted released from prisons and camps in which they were being held by the Western Powers, to help him govern the new Germany – his 'Fourth Reich'.

They would include all former Nazi leaders, particularly those who had served in the Reichstag, and their deputies. He would want all the highest state ministers and secretaries. Field marshals, generals and admirals were on the list.

'By special wish of Rudolf Hess,' he wrote, 'the former Vice President of the Reichstag, Hermann Esser, who is now in a camp in Ludwigsburg, is to be released and be given a car for fastest possible transport to Munich. Also Direktor Hofwebar, who is in the same camp, should go along in the car.' Munich, he had decided, was to be the new seat of government and the capital of Germany.

With him in Nuremberg were other men Hess needed. They should 'be told to report to me immediately', ordered Nuremberg Prisoner No. 125. They included: Reichsleiter Otto Dietrich, Hitler's former press chief; Minister Dr Schmidt; Dr Blohme; SS Obergruppenführer Pohl; Dr Martin, former police president of Nuremberg; Count Lutz; Schwerin von Krosigk; Minister Funk; State Secretary Fritz Rheinhardt; Fritz Wiedermann; Professor Dr Messerschmitt; Hess's former driver Lipert. He did not forget his imprisoned brother Alfred. He had a job for him. And he had a position for the doctor at his local hospital in Hindelang.

Hess asked for quarters in Nuremberg prison where he could 'receive a great many long-distance telephone calls, telegrams and letters'. He wanted electronic equipment set up, as well as telegraph and radio equipment at his disposal for communicating with the German people. Conference rooms should be made available too.

Occupation troops should be notified of his order that provocation by Germans would be kept to an absolute minimum. Orders should be sent off to the German railway management to give free tickets to all travellers on their way to meet him in Munich. 'If I have not the power to order the railways to do this then it must be done by the occupation forces.'

Hess's new Reichstag would number about 500 men. There would be no women. These men would of course need quarters, so garrisons would be taken over to accommodate them. 'Esser will immediately move to see the American Commandant in Munich and confer with him.'

Hess had an important job for his present prison companion Baldur von Schirach. Many buildings would be needed in Munich, and it was von Schirach's job to secure them. German police would be recruited and armed with small arms such as pistols, machine-pistols and light machine guns. They must be clothed and fed properly and be given good boots and blankets. 'I would like Reichsminister Speer,' he wrote of the man occupying a cell along the passage, 'to be assigned the job of lessening the crisis that exists in Germany. He must be given all the help necessary to set up feeding stations and transportation, to issue blankets and field kitchens. At every large railway station there should be a kitchen to give food to soldiers who are on their way home.'

Hess would of course need a limousine for himself and three accompanying cars for the trip down to Munich. One of the cars would be for Speer, the others for other important figures released from Nuremberg. 'If possible,' wrote Hess, 'I want German cars.'

Then came a personal note: 'I wish to be given back the one hundred English pounds and the several thousand Reichsmarks which I brought back with me from the United Kingdom and which were supposedly "lost" in the prison. The £100 is the payment to me as a prisoner-of-war, under the terms of the Geneva Convention.' All of his private papers should be returned to him – including his Nuremberg diaries. He would appoint a liaison man, who, he hoped, would deal with one liaison man from the Western Occupation Forces, who would have power of attorney for the others.

I have prepared releases to radio and the Press: In the name of Rudolf Hess, the following should be made known:

1. Rudolf Hess has given the Vice-President of the German Reichstag, Hermann Esser, the order to call together as soon as possible, the members of the German Reichstag. He [Hess] will then speak personally to explain the entire programme of the new government.
2. Rudolf Hess gives the order to Speer to help the German people in getting all food and kitchen equipment and transportation together. This can only be done by working together with the Allied Forces.
3. German folk police will be trained and will protect the German people from trouble-making minorities and from looting and stealing.
4. Control of Press and radio should be changed so that it speaks for the majority of the people and not for the minority. It will not be controlled as it was under Hitler where nothing appeared unless it was approved by Goebbels.

The Leader of the German folk police has been named but not written down yet. [Hess left a space for the name.]

I ask our editors who are ready for work to give me by telegram the following information: name, address and age; where and for whom they wrote; in what field they wrote – politics, economy [etc] and what title they held in their last job.

Press and radio have made attacks against former outer and inner opponents. They must stop this immediately. It is not their mission to keep old wounds open, or to open new ones.

On the order of Rudolf Hess all district gauleiters and high officials of the Nazi Parry should report to their former offices as soon as possible and take up the jobs they formerly had – members of their staffs as well.

If Jews ask or plead or request to save themselves from the rage of the German population and wish to go into protective camps this should be fulfilled. In this way everything should be done to save the Jews from acts of violence and also from unauthorized persons entering the camps.

It is up to them to make their lives as nice as possible to their own taste, within the camp. The situation in such a camp must be as humane as possible. Otherwise the occupation forces will have to be asked for food and other necessary items for the people in these camps.

All precautions should be taken by the police for the new leader's protection when he arrived at the first meeting of the Reichstag. A full guard should be mounted so that all precautions can be taken against the assassination of Rudolf Hess.

Hess had apparently no knowledge at the time of the cremation and scattered ashes of the eleven colleagues who had been condemned to death. For he wrote:

Honour guards should be put on the graves of the eleven martyrs who were hanged in Nuremberg, until they can be put into one communal grave so they can have one common honour guard. There should also be honour guards on the graves of Himmler, Ley, Rust, Hildebrand, etc. The soldiers Goering, Keitel and Jodl shall have their medals put into their caskets – certainly the Great Cross of Goering and the Ritterkreuz of the two others. Also notify their families that they can be buried in uniforms with all their ribbons. For all the others, only the Party honour badges are to be put into their graves.

Radio programmes should be no Nationalistic circus: Not too much marching music, but good music; also gay music, but no jazz and dance programmes. Certain beloved programmes should be re-introduced, also the folk concerts, with some changes. Rudolf Hess has listened to the Berlin programmes from England on the radio and found that for weeks it was the same old programmes with the old used-up pieces. It should be of a higher level than it has been to now. Rudolf Hess does not want nasty cabaret with its nasty jokes; he wants a lot of gay items, but at the same time, it should be dignified. He wishes to see the first programme before he gives it his approval …

It was too early at this stage to draw up a new constitution. The fate of the people was the important matter. 'Later the people will tell me if they are content with my leadership and will back me up as the Führer.'

I talked once about the title 'Führer' with the Führer. It went so closely with his personality that I would not find it right to use it myself too much. It should die with Adolf Hitler. Hitler wasn't for that at all. He said the title should be kept and that every one of his successors should use it.

I will fulfil this wish of the Führer for a certain time, but I cannot call myself 'Führer' until I am Führer to the whole of Germany.

Finally, he had prepared the oath his followers would swear on taking office: 'By God the Almighty, I swear to be truthful and obedient to Rudolf Hess, to perform the duties of the National Socialist Reichsrat [the lower house of parliament] to the best of my ability. And especially to be absolutely silent about any matter that has been spoken here.'

And now he had arranged his parliament, this is how he planned to address it:

TO THE MEN OF THE GERMAN REICHSTAG

I think of the dead. The dead whom our people had to sacrifice in their millions in the years of desperate struggle for its freedom and its bread.

And I think of those who died after the end of the struggle because we lost freedom, and with freedom lost our livelihood.

Above all, I think of the one among the dead: the originator and leader of the National Socialist Reich, Adolf Hitler. In my pain I feel united with them here, and with millions outside whose fidelity has remained unshaken. I think of the many men who have deserved well of people and country, who had to die because they were condemned to death; first and foremost of my eleven comrades who became the victims of the Nuremberg Trials, with the Reichsmarschall Goering at their head.

At the same time I think of all the other Germans – women, girls and boys among them, who also died in the course of the appalling judicial murders; judicial murders for which the judges were as little responsible as the condemned were for the crimes with which they were charged.

There are many gaps in your ranks, the ranks of the leaders of the Movement gathered together here in the Reichstag. Some of them fell, often in the defence of territory committed to their care, some of them voluntarily by their own hand, some of them murdered under the guise of judicial convictions. Among these are many names well known to the whole of our people and who worked with devotion for the nation in war and peace.

I think of all who in the last days of the war and after it, elected to end their own lives. I name – as representative of other wives who could not be restrained from dying with their husbands – the wife of the Führer. I think of Frau Goebbels as a mother who shared her husband's fate with five children. The mothers took their children with them when they died by their own hand, because they could no longer bear to watch them starving ...

Cruel fate decreed that the Founder of the National Socialist Reich had to die, faced by the apparent certainty that his creation was destroyed forever. The Führer died a voluntary death. He took it upon himself to die because he had no choice.

He could not expose himself to undignified treatment. He could not submit to the jurisdiction of judges who had no right to try him. Anyone else could, but he could not. He – the Head of the German State. He could not, even if he had been able to foresee the final defeat of Germany.

If he had continued to live, this would not have benefited the nation, for he would have shared the fate of those who died in the Nuremberg drama. He would thus not have been able to take part in the revival of the National Socialist Reich if he had tried to save himself for this purpose.

Nor would the Führer have been able to use the International Court for the purpose of making out a convincing case for the German cause for all the world. The more convincingly he spoke, the more mutilated would have been the reports that reached the public. Many of the accused at Nuremberg spoke very impressively – and what did the world hear? Worse still, mental pressure could also have been brought to bear on the Führer, and as a result he like other prisoners and witnesses would surely have been reduced to a condition in which he would have made false charges against Germany. He, who had the most authoritative voice of all, would have done serious harm to the Reich. All in all, the offensive treatment of the Head of the German State would have provided a spectacle which must have been intolerable to the nation. There would have been no compensating advantage.

The spectacle would have been all the more intolerable since this Head of State was one of the most significant personalities in the history of the world. And that, not as a destructive force. No. That of a creative, building or constructive force. History will one day recognize this.

The figure of the Führer will stand like a beacon over the centuries. Adolf Hitler will be honoured as one of the greatest pathfinders and benefactors of mankind.

If my captivity was decisive for the future in this respect, it was also in another respect: the desolate solitary confinement compelled me to 'think', in preparation for later 'action'. It was thanks to the lonely hours I spent in prison that I was able to collect my thoughts on the planning and carrying out of the reconstruction and on the solution of the many problems which awaited us.

I devoted myself to exhaustive thinking about the future, because I carried within me the conviction that the day would come when I would be free again, the miraculous day for our people. The 'turning' point!

This certainty was rooted in my belief in an Almighty Power which guides events in a way that makes sense and that brings each into inter relationship with each other purposefully. I knew that for the sake of a task allotted to me, I would be saved from danger of a kind I had never thought I might have to endure. It could not have been without deeper meaning that I became inured to powerful poisons, inured to the effects of mental compulsion that enabled me to recognize the existence of a secret of such decisive influence on the course of history.

The Führer once said, in a speech during the war, that the fulfilment of great tasks entailed the bearing of great sufferings. I was not spared the sufferings, physical and mental. Completely cut off from the outside world, as it were chained and gagged, I was compelled to watch how Fate dealt with my Germany. And all the time I knew that I would bring salvation if only I regained my freedom and was able to enlighten the enemy peoples as to the crimes committed against them as well and as to how they have been misused.

Since the spring of 1942, since my knowledge hardened into certainty, I knew, among other things, that Germany would lose the war and would lose it because its wartime leadership and its armaments industry would be increasingly mismanaged and would come to a standstill.

What I had foreseen came to pass. I was powerless to do anything about it or to do anything to ward it off, or even to issue any warning. I kept on making fresh plans of escape. I kept on making fresh attempts, right up to an attempt which borders on the extreme limit of what could ever be undertaken. All in vain! Each fresh plan, each fresh attempt was accompanied by the highest hopes and ended in deepest disappointment.

It was at the trial – if anywhere – that I would be able to address the public.

My statement did in fact have the effect of enabling me to continue to stand my trial. Not that I intended to defend myself; I refused to do this expressly from the very start. I went on record as saying I would not listen. I disputed the court's right to sit in judgement on Germans. On the other hand, I aimed to make use of the framework of the trial as the forum before which to make my accusation in the eyes of the world.

However, steps had been taken to prevent this. My revelations could only be convincingly presented in the course of a long speech; I was prevented from having a chance to do this. The statement regarding my memory would probably require only a few sentences. I wanted to use the answer to the question of whether I felt myself to be guilty – the answer was restricted to 'Yes' or 'No'. I tried to get permission to speak independently. This was ruled to be out of order.

Both my defence counsel and some of my fellow accused had been trying for weeks to persuade me to desist from making a final statement. 'Keeping silent,' they said, 'would be an impressive demonstration.'

They only stopped acting like this when I appeared to agree. When I then nevertheless made use of my right, one of my fellow accused kept on talking throughout my speech in an attempt to confuse me and to break my train of thought; he urged me to stop, although he must have been aware that my conclusively proved revelations could be of immeasurable importance for his fate and that of his fellow sufferers. And indeed for the faith of the nation.

The majority of the accused were clearly likewise under the influence of the external coercive agent.

The executions resulting from the Nuremberg Trials are judicial murders. The judges were aware of this. After the death sentences had been passed, I clung to the hope that the miracle of the great turn of the tide of Fate would occur before the sentences were carried out. In vain.

Perhaps the enormity of executing completely innocent persons, some of whom bore names of world renown, had to be enacted before the eyes of humanity, in order that humanity should recognize fully, how immeasurably great the crimes and how unscrupulous the criminals were.

The repercussions of the death of the eleven will be as great as those of their martyrdom. For they did in fact suffer martyrdom. Everything that could be done to break the prisoners' nerve and to increase their mental anguish was done. They nevertheless maintained in the highest degree a manly bearing and suffered their bitter fate with heads unbowed. Torn hither and thither for months on end between hope and despair, but never breaking down, they all faced what seemed to them a certain fate with admirable courage. For weeks on end they looked certain death in the eye. Upright, they took the last hard road to their death, each one of them a hero.

Only one of them – Hermann Goering – kept the means of anticipating execution at the last moment by committing suicide. The fury and disappointment shown by the opponents of the German people, as evidenced in the Press and radio, confirm how right he was to act as he did to prevent the intended spectacle of the hanging of the German Reichsmarschall. The effect of the appalling treatment meted out to my fellow prisoners must have been all the greater since I was unable to convince them that their captors were insane.

I on the other hand was sure of this. I was thus able to brush off all efforts to insult me or to break down my resistance, as being the behaviour of pitiful, sick persons into whose hands I had for the time being fallen.

I am, in principle, of the opinion that a person's honour cannot be injured by actions or utterances of another person. Anyone who attempts to do this injures his own honour. A person's honour can only be harmed by dishonourable behaviour on the part of the person concerned.

In this connection I wish to make the following statement: My defence counsel entered an appeal for a revision of the judgement found against me. It was then put about that I had made an appeal for 'mercy': In the first place an appeal from judgement is not a plea for mercy; secondly, my defence counsel's action was taken without my knowledge and against my will.

Behind hunger, cold, murder and despair, Bolshevism raises its ugly head. It is only with the Bolshevization of Europe that the objective would be reached, which was the purpose of the war. The rule of Bolshevism is the rule of the Jew.

Two world wars and twice the same result: Jewish power increased. Does it need much political farsightedness to recognize that World War III is already being prepared? The new world war. This time the fronts will be, on one side the Bolshevists, and on the other the Anglo-Saxons. Who will win? That side will win in whose favour the secret agency is employed.

The real instrument of power in the hands of the Jew is the Bolshevist. It is proved by the fact that for years a Jew has been at the head of the research department of the United States Atomic Power Organization. Is anyone going to believe that this Jew, hitherto completely unknown among scientists, has suddenly been put in this high position where all the secrets relating to the future war must be available? The atom bomb will be the main weapon of the Jewish-Bolshevist war leadership in spite of the fact that it is also in British and American hands.

The Soviet Union will probably use it first and be able to destroy everything in the West. They have the best possible excuse for doing so because they can say the West used it first. The Anglo-Saxon countries will be the first to go under – I, Rudolf Hess, have warned you!

Fresh from his manifesto writing, Hess sketched a hand-drawn diagram of taps and piping showing how the water flow into the shower attached to his cell could be improved. He then opened another page in his notebook to write an essay – illustrated by two columns of dates – equating the milestones in Hitler's career and the similarity with Napoleon's, 130 years apart. In 1810 Napoleon was master of Europe; in 1940 so was Hitler. In 1812 the retreat from Moscow took place, said Hess. At the end of 1942 the siege of Moscow was doomed, as was the Nazi invasion of the USSR. And the 1815 finale of one tyrant coincided 130 years later in 1945 as the vanquishing of another.

As Hess was writing his manifesto, French nerve specialist Dr Andre Guibert had made an assessment of the mood of the Spandau prison and its seven newly arrived inhabitants.

I saw the prisoners all walking in the garden; they all wore US Army greatcoats with numbers on their backs. The coats had been dyed. I immediately thought back to the time of glory that they had once experienced; and the contrast of them now, being the most disgraced men on earth, and among the most hated. I thought of the enormous staff each of them had and their position and relationship with Hitler; the responsibilities that they had in that great dream of conquering the world. Here they were – these lonely men who had just escaped death: the gallows at Nuremberg.

CHAPTER 12

ON THE BRINK OF WAR

he carton of garage papers yielded even more; the Berlin Blockade – which was to last from 21 June 1948 to 11 May 1949 – had then begun. The Soviet Union had blocked railway and street access to West Berlin, and even though the crisis abated after the Soviets made no move to stop American, British and French airlifts of food and other provisions to the Western-held sectors of Berlin, the tension around the Spandau directors' table was high.

On 22 July 1948 a confidential US Intelligence report to the Allied directors of the prison warned: 'Since the suspension of the meetings of the Allied Kommandatur [the Joint Command of the Allied Powers in Berlin], the Spandau Prison is about the only activity still operating on a quadripartite basis in Germany. One of several possibilities may ensue:

A: The Soviets may withdraw their exterior military guards without any incidents. B: The Soviets may refuse to withdraw their military guard at the appointed time, August 1, 1948, on the pretext that the Western Allies can no longer be trusted with the safeguarding of the prisoners or were furnishing inadequate guards. A policy decision is required on what our action should be in this event. We must remember that the Spandau Allied Prison is located in the British Sector and the Soviets may use these installations as a pretext to concentrate a large number of armed troops there to 'safeguard the prisoners'. C: The Soviets may elect to withdraw entirely from any further participation with the quadri-partite administration of the prison. In such an event, the three western powers must arrive at a policy decision as to whether they continue to operate on a quadripartite basis or close the prison and transfer the prisoners to one of the zones, perhaps to the Nuremberg prison from whence they came.

Or the Soviets may forcibly seize control of the prison and may remove the prisoners from Berlin into their control. This again would demand a policy decision by the western powers as to the desired action of such an eventuality. From a practical standpoint it would appear that the three western powers might not be in a position militarily to pre-vent the use of force by Soviet military forces as such action could lead to war.

Despite the Berlin situation being at danger-point, the Spandau directors' meetings were often as mundane as normal. The four directors were pon-derously discussing the disposition of garden produce, care and storage of gardening tools in the gardening shed and the election of the French direc-tor as gardening supremo.

At his cell table Rudolf Hess was writing to his wife:

Education as market gardeners makes rapid progress. It is voluntary, but we all take part. I am already quite an expert in tomato growing. I know which shoots to nip off and which to take away. When the stems of pruned shoots are stuck into the ground the moisture is retained better and the unwanted parts convert themselves into good manure.

In a following letter to Ilse:

I am not surprised that my tomato pruning caused you amusement. In between, I did some tobacco pruning too. As a non-smoker I found it rather unfair that I should be expected to look after and gather these plants so that the slaves of nicotine could fill themselves with poison.

He went on to explain how far carrots should be set in the soil; the relative growth of onions, cucumber, cauliflower and kohlrabi; and for the first time gathering walnuts from prison trees – 'tens of thousands of them'.

The only one of us who knows anything about the job is our doyen, Herr von Neurath, and for this reason is head director of gardening operations.

On 9 May 1948 – the day before another anniversary of his flight to Scotland – Hess wrote again to his wife: 'Tomorrow evening will mark the seventh year that I have spent in imprisonment.'

When it began, I thought it might last seven hours. As soon as I made myself known to the Duke [of Hamilton] and explained my mission as a parlementar [officer bearing the flag of truce] I assumed that I would be treated in the manner that a parlementar ought to be treated – even if I came as a self-appointed one. When it became apparent that I had deceived myself in this respect I reckoned with seven days until the matter was taken up officially.

Well! I had to learn to stretch the thread of hope toward the day of liberty – to stretch it more and more! I did not want to return without having done my job. In the very first days I said to one of the officers about me, that the worst thing they could do to me was to ship me off home then and there. Whereupon, the good man became 'all ears' and opened wide his mouth and eyes in expectancy of 'the revelation' that the people over there awaited; namely that I had escaped from Nazi Germany with the reasons thrown in. However he was visibly disappointed when I assured him that the object of my flight was not to practise long-distance flying and navigation; to satisfy an ambition to break through the British defence system; to enjoy the sensation of parachute-jumping in Scotland; or possibly to make an overseas trip to Portugal – all the while certain of being shot or imprisoned at home without first of all speaking to somebody in high authority in England and, at the very least, putting my suggestion before him.

After the parlaying was over, the situation would be different; then I myself would lay wait until I could return home as fitting for a parlementar. At that time I had not the faintest idea of what – in any positive sense – would be the meaning of my being retained as a prisoner.

The compass within my breast had guided me as surely as a precise navigation compass guides to the north. Or the compass of my good old ME110 all the way to my destination.

Hess divulged to his wife that Ernst Udet (a veteran First World War fighter pilot and at the time a general in the Luftwaffe), was 'in' on his flight and would soothe Hitler by saying it was

out of the question that I would achieve my goal. Either I would fall into the sea because with so little practice I would not be able to manage such a complicated machine; or I would vanish somewhere over the ocean. Or in spite of all this, if I did reach the British Isles, it was absolutely certain I would be shot down. If that didn't happen, I would infallibly break my neck in trying to bale out. But – as I have already written – the Führer completely differed from Udet; he was pessimistic enough to feel sure that once I had got a thing thoroughly into my head and wrestled with it, I would not fail to carry it out.

Well, he was right. He knew his deputy better and longer than all the others – and as for the political consequences which caused him serious anxiety, he was content to leave things in the hands of Fate. Frank told me in Nuremberg that Hitler had told him afterwards that I must have made such an uncompromising decent impression on the English that even they would not feel able – even in the middle of a war – to make capital of my flight; to issue false reports as to my purpose – as he had expected them to do.

On my part, I had assumed that this same uncompromising decency would be met with the same qualities. I had not calculated far enough to realise that Churchill no longer had the power to act freely, or to check the avalanche then sliding down upon us.

'There you are,' he concluded. 'Those are a few memories from the past touching on the seven-year Jubilee of my act of "indiscretion".'

Another insight into Hess's flight came from an interview with Willi Messerschmitt, reported by the Dena news agency, as he waited to be called as a witness during the trial. He said it was in 1940, at Augsburg, that Hess first approached him with the request that he be allowed to test new fighter aircraft.

Messerschmitt said at first he refused Hess's request. Hess insisted his 'position' gave him the right to fly the new ME 110, and finally he gave in. Hess – who Messerschmitt described as 'an excellent pilot' – undertook some twenty flights from Augsburg airfield. After each flight he told Messerschmitt and his engineers of faults he claimed he had found in the machines.

'On 10 May, 1941, Hess appeared in officer's uniform without badges of rank, at flight control, and under his wife's maiden name signed off for a flight from Augsburg to Stavanger in Norway. There he joined a bomber formation which flew to England – in itself a difficult undertaking for an amateur.'

Messerschmitt said the first he knew of the Hess flight was when he was in a pub at Innsbruck when Goering phoned and ordered him to Munich for an interview. Next morning he waited on Goering in his special train at Munich station.

'He was wearing one of his fancy-dress uniforms; he pointed with his marshall's baton at my stomach and yelled at me: "As far as you're concerned it seems that anyone can take off with a Messerschmitt!"

'I asked him what he meant by that. He said: "You know – this chap Hess."

'I said: "Yes, but Hess isn't just anybody!" Goering then calmed down. He said: "You should have made enquiries before you put a machine at the disposal of a man like that."

'I replied: "If you were to come to my works and ask for a machine, ought I first apply to the Führer for permission?"

'This made Goering furious again. And he barked at me: "That's not the same thing at all! I'm the Air Minister."

'And I replied: "And Hess is the Führer's deputy."

'Goering said: "But you should have been aware, Messerschmitt, that this man was mad!"

'To which I could only reply dryly: "How could I assume that a madman could occupy such a high position in the Third Reich? You, Herr Reichsmarschall, should have persuaded him to resign."

'Goering laughed out loud and said: "Oh, there's no getting around you, Messerschmitt! Trot along and keep on turning out your aircraft. I promise you I'll give you a helping hand if the Reichsführer should take it into his head to treat you badly in this matter."'

CHAPTER 13

THAT CUNNING CHURCHILL

Hess's assessment of Winston Churchill's inability 'to check the avalanche' was made in ignorance of what really occupied the Prime Minister's mind. Churchill took until 19 May 1941 to decide how best to use the deputy Führer's astonishing flight. He decided to send a small group of colleagues – headed by Lord Simon, who knew Hess personally – to 'use' Hess in bogus 'negotiations' for an understanding between Britain and Germany, frightening the Russians into believing Germany was about to attack.

Hess said Simon met him on 9 June and they signed a four-point declaration summarising Hess's ideas for peace – which could be shown to the Russians.

Hess wrote (in a statement discovered by Gene Bird in 1970, in the cardboard box sent from Nuremberg):

It was my hope to be able to convince the British Government how senseless it was to continue this war until both sides were exhausted and brought to the verge of breakdown.

At the same time, I wanted to give the British Government an opportunity to make a declaration on the following lines: 'As a result of discussions with Rudolf Hess, the Government now feel that the Führer's offers are sincerely meant. In these circumstances it would be irresponsible to continue the bloodshed without ourselves trying to reach an understanding. We therefore declare our readiness to negotiate.'

'It was in this sense,' Hess wrote, 'that I explained the purpose of my mission to the Duke of Hamilton the day after I had landed. At the same time I explained how the Führer felt.

'I also informed the then Lord Chancellor, Simon, in the course of a two-hour discussion which took place on 9 June, 1941, at the instigation of the British Government. On this occasion I put forward as a basis for negotiation, the above-mentioned two points, which I added two further points, namely:

3. Restitution to be made for injury or loss incurred by the Germans living in British territory and by British subjects in German territory, on a reciprocal basis.

4. Armistice and peace to be concluded with Italy simultaneously.

I incorporated these four points in a document which I signed. At the end of the discussion Lord Simon assured me he would make a full report to his Government.

I never received an answer. For more than two years the public remained in ignorance of the fact that a discussion had taken place. It was not until the end of September, 1943, that the then British Foreign Minister, Eden, announced that I had on the occasion of a discussion on 9th June, 1941, in a document I had handed over, put forward six points as 'conditions of peace'. He thus added two points to my four.

I here and now state categorically that in the discussion and in the document I referred only to the four points mentioned.

This is corroborated by the minutes of the discussion which we handed to me and the transfer copy of the document which remained in my hands. The German witness, whose presence I had stipulated, can likewise confirm this fact. In the course of the discussion I, myself, made no mention of the points added by Mr Eden. One of the alleged 'conditions' that I was supposed to have laid down, related to 'claims which Germany was said to have on Russia'. It was further alleged that the fulfilment of these demands would have to be achieved by negotiation, and if this proved impossible, would have to be settled by war.

Any such statement made shortly before the German action against Soviet Russia would have been tantamount to treason. I assume that the purpose of spreading this falsehood was to break the nerve of a prisoner who was not in a position to defend himself in the eyes of the world. Nevertheless, I do not make Mr. Eden any reproach on this account for reasons which today need no longer be gone into.

Hess was under no delusion regarding the Russian threat to Germany. 'In November, 1940, the Führer told me that he wanted to inform me about his plans for the next year. I asked him to please let me state, uninfluenced first, what I would do if I were in his place. I expressed my conviction that Soviet Russia had signed the non-aggression treaty with us only to soothe us, and to enable her to attack us, with better chance of success, at a moment convenient to her.'

Three months later Hess was in his cell writing to Ilse once more: 'Before I forget! Let me answer your query about the suggested visit at once. It is meant – I know – very kindly. But I do not wish to have any visits, unimportant or otherwise. I cannot give you all my reasons for this decision, and some of them have already been given.' He returned to news of his gardening. 'This year I am not specialising in tomatoes, but in turnips and marigolds.'

In August 1948 trouble was brewing between the already jittery directors – not about the possibility of war, but Russian discipline restricting the feeding of the seven prisoners. The Soviet director alleged that on three occasions during the US month of control, food in excess of authorised rations had been served. The Russian said he had personally weighed the supper served to Hess and his fellow prisoners and discovered that it was 500 grams in excess of the allowable amount for summer. The US director argued that the 1,999 calories allowed per day per prisoner was not practical to be divided equally between three meals and the Russian's 'weigh-in' bore little relationship to the facts. Also the prisoners' weights had not materially changed in that month. He said the Russian's actions in the kitchen in the presence of United Nations personnel and other employees were 'highly discourteous and out of order'. The Soviet director told the meeting that while he was weighing the prisoners' food, the American warder Mikesh was discourteous and disrespectful to him and should be severely disciplined. The US director replied that because of the Soviet director's own discourtesy, there would be no discipline for Mikesh. The Russian then said he would report this to his superiors. The US director said any report he desired to make 'would be welcome'.

As it had been re-enacted for years, the changing of the guard at the grim old prison proceeded as it had always done. At 12 noon precisely, on the first day of the month, guards lined up in platoon formation, three 'reliefs' in formation on the left-hand side of the courtyard; the fourth relief of seven soldiers on post to be relieved by the incoming nation. When the US was taking over from the Russians, a platoon of thirty-seven US soldiers in full-dress duty uniform marched in to face the Russians. Weapons were then brought down and the departing Russian officer announcing (in Russian): 'In the name of the Soviet Union I hereby relinquish the security of Spandau Allied Prison.' The Soviet officer of the day would take a key to open the door, the US guard would march inside and the guard on each tower exchanged.

Inside the directors' offices the mood had deteriorated. In December 1948, upset with the Soviets' harshness, Col. Frank Howley, Commandant of the Office of the US Military Government, Berlin Sector, sent a memo to the US director of the prison.

It has come to my attention that we, as representatives of the US, are guilty in permitting certain inhumane treatments of war criminals who are now interned in Spandau Prison. It appears – that due to Russian obstruction and Russian vetoing and Russian interference in the prison – we have been unable, even in the months of American chairmanship, to carry out the prison agreements in a humane manner and in the spirit in which the agreements were originally made.

Therefore you will immediately put into effect the following measures:

You will liberally, and in a humane manner, interpret these agreements which have been signed by us and by the other three Powers concerned with the care of these prisoners. Those changes in the diet which were authorised, whereby those prisoners suffering from diabetes were to be given substitutes; whereby those suffering from anaemia were to be given small quantities of additional food to take care of their health condition – are immediately put into effect during our chairmanship. The purpose of this additional food will be to arrest the deteriorating physical condition of the prisoners who are continuing to lose weight under the present harsh conditions and who are approaching a point beyond that of expectable malnutriton.

You will permit prisoners when in their cells to sit or lie in their beds as they see fit at any hour of day or night.

You will permit prisoners to speak with each other within reasonable limits when they are together. For security reasons conversations should be checked to ensure that they are not of a political or security-threatening nature. You will permit prisoners to have one visitor for 15 minutes every two months. In fact, where it is psychologically desirable, more frequent visitors, possibly one per month for 30 minutes. The visitors will be permitted to bring two food packages, each package not to exceed two kilos in weight, and no prisoner to receive more than two packages per month. You will permit prisoners to receive at least one letter every four weeks. This may be increased if any prisoner so desires, to allow for the receipt and posting of one letter each week. Your censorship of outgoing and incoming letters will be only to the extent of ensuring essential security. No attempt to interfere with the normal phrasing of personal letters will be made.

You will provide a minimal amount of recreational facilities as determined by the US medical advisor, Col. Chamberlin. This recreation will be consistent with normal prison practice and could possibly include 'horseshoes' for outdoor exercise as well as magazines or books of a non-political or non-security nature; possibly even checkers which would require two prisoners, under supervision, to relieve their monotony which otherwise contributes to mental and physical deterioration.

[And in regards to Russian interference with the regulations:] It is desirable that these acts be in accordance with the desires of the French, British and Russian directors. However – I will not permit this order to be vetoed by Russian obstruction or Russian delay. During the American chairmanship these measures will be taken. They will become effective as at 1200 hrs today, 2 December, 1948. And effort will be made to persuade the British, French and Russian directors to follow this time of humane treatment during their chairmanship, though I recognise the possible limitation of your influence, particularly over the Russian director.

The prisoners most in need of specific diets were Funk (diabetes, urinary retention and cystitis); Doenitz (malnutrition and vitamin deficiency); and Raeder (malnutrition, hypertension and cardiac decompensation).

Next day the Soviet representative, told of the US memo, said he would report 'this unilateral action' to his superiors and when he had a reaction, would inform the directors of its contents.

A cell inspection took place, after which it was reported that each of the seven cells had an army cot with a mattress and blankets, a table, chair and WC. Prisoners were allowed photographs of their family on the walls. One cell was transformed into a library with 300 books, some the personal property of the prisoners; Raeder was appointed librarian. About 150 books were exchanged each month at the Spandau Public Library. Each prisoner was allowed a Bible and three other books in his cell. Another cell had been made into a small chapel containing five seats, a harmonium, altar and Christmas or Advent decorations. The French chaplain conducted church services and Funk played the organ. All prisoners attended the services except Hess who would not go to church. Apart from the four directors there was a staff of 32 warders, 18 United Nations displaced persons working inside the cell-house proper, and a staff of 52 Germans working outside the cell-block, forbidden to approach any of the prisoners within speaking distance.

Increased sabre-rattling between the Allied directors and the Soviet director resulted in an angry confrontation in early January 1949. It was the British control month and the British director decided to put the American advisory into practice, giving the kitchen its directions. The Soviet director bristled: 'I object! But if the chairman sees fit to adopt this measure over my objection there is nothing that can be done about it.' Nevertheless, the Allies met later to discuss their concern about what would actually happen when it was time for the Russians to take charge. They came up with the possibilities:

The imposition by the Soviets of drastically harsh measures in the prison-
ers' treatment, resulting in irreparable damage to some of them.
Removal of the prisoners from Spandau.
Refusal to allow Western representatives to enter the prison.
Refusal to remove the military guard from Spandau on the expiration of
the Russian chairmanship.

But what could the Western powers do about it? They could not interfere
with the Soviet system provided it was within the new regulations; they
could take advantage of the three periods out of four of the eight hours
each when Allied warders were in the majority, and smuggle food packages to the prisoners; allow prisoners to rest or exercise; this, it was thought,
could well provoke incidents if members of the Soviet external guard were
brought into the cell-block to ensure observance of the orders issued by the
Soviet director.

Finally – a drastic last-ditch move could be made: to move the prisoners
in an Allied month to a different building in the Western sector of Berlin,
denying the Soviets any participation in their control; to fly them out to a
Western zone of Germany; or informing the Soviets that Spandau was to be
closed and that the prisoners would be handed over to the Allied power by
which they had been captured.

At a press conference on 31 January 1949, the US director told reporters that so far there had been no attempt by any German to get in touch
with any of the prisoners, surreptitious or overt, and there had been no
attempt to free any of them. None of the seven had so far attempted suicide.
There had been a chapel set up and the French chaplain who was fluent in
German conducted services, 'though I am not in a position to know what
their spiritual thoughts might be'. He said the prisoners were permitted to
busy themselves writing their memoirs, but they did not appear to keep
diaries of any sort. Memoir-writing involved yet another Allied-Soviet disa-
greement. When Speer formally requested permission to write his memoirs
the Soviet director protested:

The order is laid down by the Military Tribunal and the Regulations of
Spandau and none of these documents provides that the prisoners may

write their memoirs about their former activities. Moreover, for my part, I consider that these memoirs will have no value as the International Military Tribunal, in the course of the trial, showed the criminal activity of the main war criminals and it was written down in the trial documents. I cannot agree.

While Britain, France and the US had no objections, the item was dropped from that day's meeting agenda. The Russian objections made no difference to Speer. He was writing his memoirs and had them smuggled out of the jail by an 'unknown' helper – said by Col. Bird to have been a Dutch male nurse who had been a forced hospital labourer under the Germans. When he was released from Spandau, Speer had 25,000 pages of his secret diary written in his cell, most of it on sheets of toilet paper which he kept hidden in his shoes until they could be smuggled out of the prison to await his release. He said in an introduction to his bestseller 450-page book, *Spandau: the Secret Diaries*:

> these thousands of notes are one concentrated effort to survive and not only to endure life in a cell, physically and intellectually, but also to arrive at some sort of moral reckoning with what lay behind it all.

For some time real toilet paper was not given to the prisoners. Each was given an allocation of small packets of newspapers cut into squares. Uncomfortable as newsprint might have been, it gave the seven an opportunity to read what was going on in the outside world, at the time forbidden.

Five of the ex-Nazis smoked; Hess and Raeder did not. The smokers were allowed pipes and a tobacco ration, but not cigarettes. Von Schirach liked English Dunhill pipes and one was sent to him with a chrome mouthpiece. The Russians protested that this was a luxury item so he was not allowed to have it. The pipe was put away on a shelf to await his release. Soap could be sent in – so long as it was not perfumed. Again, said the Russians, perfumed soap was considered a luxury item. What was not available in the Soviet Union was a 'luxury'.

Gene Bird said handling Soviet obstinacy in the prison needed skill:

There was always great tension between the directors, particularly during the Cold War. It was always possible to sense the overall political situation as reflected around the directors' table in the prison. A lot depends on how you associate with these Russians; how you approach them. Once a Russian says 'no', there is no way you're going to change his mind. His superior might, eventually, but he will not. You must be careful not to back him into a corner. Never pin him down too tightly. Always leave a way open for him. Maybe work around him a little to get what you want. If you play your cards open you can get results.

During the blockade this was the only place we (of the West) could meet the Russians. They had walked out of every other place. But they stayed on at Spandau. Even Kruschev was saying: 'There is evidence in the world that representatives of the Four Powers can sit down and work together and get along together – and for that I point to Spandau Allied Prison in Berlin.' The Russian director proudly brought in the newspaper quoting him. There was very little actual negotiation at Spandau during the Cold War, but the prison was used to get messages across to 'the other side'.

One afternoon a British guard's machine gun was accidentally discharged and the bullet narrowly missed the head of the Soviet director. The Soviets immediately accused the British of trying to kill their man.

The weights of the seven prisoners were recorded. Doenitz had been 64.7 kg and was now 61.6; von Neurath had been 67.8 when he arrived and was now 64.5; Raeder's weight had dropped only slightly from 55.6 to 55.5; Speer had been 78 kilos and was now 73; Funk had dropped from 67.4 to 64.5 kg; Hess from 66.1 to 63 kg and von Schirach from 65.2 to 61.2. They had lost weight in the French month and remained steady in the Russian month. By mid-June 1949, von Schirach had put on 2.9 kg, Doenitz 1.3, von Neurath 1.4, Raeder 3.1, Speer 1.3, Funk 0.2, and Hess 2.1 kg.

One by one, six were released between 1955 and 1966; Speer and von Schirach being released together, leaving only Hess.

On the eve of their release – which was a British month – the British general wanted to know every detail of their transport, their destination, where they were going to stay and who was going to meet them. Carrying a baton under his arm, the general went to his cell and quizzed von Schirach on his arrangements.

Von Schirach said stiffly: 'General, as of 12 midnight tomorrow I will be a free man. And it is up to me where I stay and where I want to stay.'

'About a dozen people had accompanied the general and the situation was a little embarrassing,' recalled Col. Bird.

'The general tapped von Schirach on the chest with his baton and said: "Mister, as of right now you are still a prisoner. And when you leave this prison you will still be in my sector of an occupied Berlin. So it is my business whether or not you be a free man, I am responsible for your safe being. I am responsible for you until you fly out of Berlin. I *want to know* – and I expect to know."

'After this everybody cleared out and I went to see von Schirach.

'"Why are you so arrogant?" I asked him. "Why did you answer the British general like that and embarrass him in the way you did? You had no business doing that. You know his interest was on your behalf."

'Von Schirach looked at me and said: "Colonel, I'll tell you one thing. I know this is a weakness of mine; I know it is. I've always got to tell myself: 'Now, Baldur, calm down! Get your feet back on the ground.' You see, I have never yet seen a man that I looked up to; to include Hitler or anyone else. I always feel superior in my thinking to anyone else that I've ever met."

'Here was a man, standing in prison clothes, in a cell with No. 1 painted on each knee, talking down to a magnificent British general!

'Von Schirach always started straight in with his requests, whether he was talking to a guard or a general. Speer would greet the general as though they were at a cocktail party.'

Months before he was due to go free, von Schirach had feared he was going blind. Col. Bird reported to the other directors on 26 January 1965:

I was informed by phone this morning that yesterday afternoon von Schirach had trouble with his right eye. The British Director was summoned and he directed that a patch be put over the eye, that von Schirach should go to bed and his cell be darkened. Next day a routine medical examination revealed he had an extensive detachment of the retina. An eye specialist from the US Army Hospital was called for immediate treatment and a British consultant ophthalmologist was brought from West Germany for consultation. At a special meeting it was agreed to transfer von Schirach to the British Military Hospital for an eye operation. The prisoner dictated a telegram which was sent out to his son, Klaus, by phone at 1905 hours. It read: 'Your Father is being transferred to the British Military Hospital where an eye operation will eventually be performed for a detached retina of the right eye. Visits will take place as usual. Dates will be made known. There is no cause for alarm. – Signed Prison Directorate.'

Bird's report continued: 'The doctor, Lt. Col. Milne, said that the retinal detachment was due to myopic degeneration. Even with treatment the prognosis is poor. It is quite possible that a retinal detachment will develop in the left eye.'

On 11 March 1965, on the directors' agenda, stood an item – *Hess Punishment*. 'The directors decided to deprive Hess of reading the newspapers for two days as a result of his insolence against the French warder, Mr Slowik. Hess will also be warned that in the future he will be punished for every infraction of the prison rules. The directors agreed that the records received by his family will be handed over to Speer after being played by the censors.'

8 April 1965: 'The directors took note of a letter of appreciation from von Schirach, expressing his gratitude for the manner he was cared for during his recent stay in the British Military Hospital. The directors agreed that he be allowed to stay 30 minutes longer in the garden for the duration of this month. They further agreed that Speer be allowed to read to von Schirach for 30 minutes in the forenoon and Hess to do so for 30 minutes in the afternoon.'

9 April 1965: 'On this day the Soviet Director informed me [Col. Bird reports] that we were feeding the prisoners too well. He reminded me that they should not be treated "like kings or ministers". He objected to the presence of a low chair that was placed in the cell of von Schirach. The purpose of the low chair is to allow the prisoner to sit and place his leg in an elevated position by placing it on his bed while sitting in the chair. He made

a strong point (though rather hesitatingly) that I had violated an ethic in not getting the approval of all the other directors prior to having the chair put in his cell. I also delivered a copy of *Playboy* magazine to Col. Lazarev (Soviet Director). He accepted it with thanks and said: "I do not have much to give you, as you know, but please accept this." And he gave me a tin of crab-meat.'

20 April 1965: 'Von Schirach was doing well but has experienced a flashing of light in his good (left) eye which could indicate that the procedure could be starting in the left eye. I requested that our head eye specialist should come to Berlin for further examination of the eye. He did, and examined it extensively. A degeneration has been found to be occurring. Speer needs new lenses and frames for his eyeglasses and Hess a new set of frames.'

27 April 1965: 'The right eye now seems beyond repair. The Soviet Director objected to my suggestion that we have Professor Meyer Schwickerath, a German specialist, operate. He pointed out that prison regulations state that only medical men of the Four Powers treat any of the three prisoners. I then asked the Soviet Director to have his eye doctor examine von Schirach as soon as possible. Whereupon he answered that he did not have such a specialist available. At 2.45 pm on 28th April, I received word from the Spandau directors' mess that von Schirach was experiencing seeing black spots in the remaining good eye.'

6 May 1965: 'Approval has been given for Professor Meyer Schwickerath, the Essen eye specialist, to come to Berlin and examine von Schirach. He would be transferred by ambulance to the West End Hospital in Berlin's Charlottenburg. There would be an armed guard of two British military policemen. A radio-telephone car would be in front. At the clinic the chief British Medical Officer would be present and the British military police on guard on the floor of the treatment room. Every effort would be made to prevent the Press from getting within photographing distance of the prisoner when entering or leaving the clinic. Civilian police in uniform and civilian clothes would keep watch and assist where necessary. No stranger would be allowed to make contact with the prisoner.'

8 May 1965: 'The prisoner was seen by the specialist who reported almost complete detachment of the retina of the right eye. In the left eye there was

severe destruction of vitrious body and equitorial degeneration and a clear circular hole surrounded by an earlier detachment.

'It was agreed that the operation would take place at the Westend Hospital. Von Schirach climbed into the ambulance to make what the directors believed would be the prisoner's secret trip outside the prison. But as von Schirach got out of the ambulance with his armed escort, a woman wearing a white jacket, a stethoscope round her neck and a transistor radio in her hand, approached. She said her name was Mrs Karen Stein and she wanted to give the prisoner the radio. She was a middle-aged attractive lady. She then stepped closer and announced that she wanted to donate her eyes to "her lover".'

Von Schirach was hurried into the hospital, given local anaesthetic to deaden the nerves around the eye, and clamps were attached to open the area. All four directors were present and watched as the doctor fired about seventy laser beams into the eye. When it was over von Schirach was taken back to the ambulance which travelled slowly to the British Military Hospital. Karen Stein, who had been waiting outside, made several attempts to visit the patient, even (she claimed) crawling up a tree to look into his room.

12 June 1965: 'Professor Meyer Schwickerath visited von Schirach and declared the operation had been successful. Von Schirach was brought back to Spandau and exempted from heavy work; he will be examined every month by Professor Kleeberger. Von Schirach told Warder Fowler: "I will not allow any eye specialist other than Prof. Meyer Schwickerath or Kleeberger to examine my eye."'

11 August 1965: 'Hess was visited by his lawyer, Dr Seidl. This was the second visit Hess has had in his entire period as a prisoner in over 24 years,' wrote Col. Bird. 'I attended the visit, with the Soviet director, Lazarev. Prior to the visit I cautioned Seidl to hold his conversation to legal matters only, and not to act as an intermediary between the Hess family and the prisoner. I warned him not to release anything regarding the visit to the Press afterwards; warning that if he did, he may not be allowed to see the prisoner ever again. Seidl agreed and the visit lasted 30 minutes.

'Hess complained that whereas he felt well today, he was not well at all. He was getting "pretty old". He further stated that prison confinement was slowly "doing him under". He complained that his wife and son were not responding regularly or promptly enough regarding the purchase of books. He further complained he had not received an answer to a birthday greeting he had recently sent his mother-in-law.

'The elderly Seidl, who had appeared for him at Nuremberg, again went over the Nuremberg indictments with Hess. He had been found guilty of the common plan of conspiracy and two crimes against humanity. Seidl said he felt that Count 2 was a miscarriage of justice and should be rescinded. If Hess was guilty of this charge (said Seidl) then so were De Gaulle of France and Eden of England for the part they played in the recent Suez crisis. If Hess was guilty, then De Gaulle and Eden should be brought to trial for the same charge. At this point the Soviet director objected and the visit ended. Seidl said he would write on the above subject to the heads of the Soviet, British, French and US governments.'

17 August 1965: the directors noted 'Speer is allowed four hours or more in his garden. Von Schirach could spend as much time outside, if he took a rake or other garden tool in his hand. Even if he did not actually "work" with these tools.'

30 August 1965: 'Klaus von Schirach, also acting as his Father's lawyer, visited von Schirach. His Father wanted to make it clear, he said, that: "I am being treated well at the prison. The food is excellent. The prison directorate, I know, is doing the best they can for me. I am checked regularly by the best military eye specialists available to the Four Powers. I get enough exercise in the garden each day. I am not required to work. In general, my condition is excellent, but it is very difficult for a man who is threatened by blindness to live under strict prison confinement."

'He warned his son to be careful not to release anything to the Press that sounded sensational. Klaus replied: "Papi, you can be assured that I think about it one hundred times before I take any sort of action as your lawyer. I try to do the same for you as I do for any of my clients."

'On his 11th October 1965 visit, Klaus von Schirach asked his Father: "Father, listen carefully and answer this question: Are you allowed to eat with a knife, fork and spoon?"

'Von Schirach: "That is a very odd question! It really has no bearing on my eye. I have eaten only with a spoon for the past 19 years. You know that. Since my last examination I have not gotten worse. I do have the light flickers from time to time, but aside from that, nothing new. I believe the worsening of my left eye will develop slowly and not as dramatically as my right eye."

'Klaus: "Father, as you know, I have written to the four Heads of State asking if they would consider your pardon at this time. I have not received an answer from the Soviet Union; but I have here copies of those sent to me by the French, British and the US. All three letters are exact, almost to the comma and period; all three are signed by the same person, not in too high a position. All three letters state that it is the Soviet Union that blocks your release."'

On 29 September 1966, Speer and von Schirach were getting ready to be released the next day; their sentences ended. The Russians were determined not to show compassion in any way. Bird suggested driving the two prisoners out of the jail and straight to an aircraft at Tempelhof earlier to avoid the hordes of waiting press. No, said the Russians. They were major war criminals and should not be released one second before their sentences had been served.

And – said the Soviet director – they must wear the same clothes they wore when they were arrested. Bird protested: 'This is impossible! Speer was arrested wearing an old ski jacket, pants and ski boots all 20 years old. Von Schirach came in wearing an old pair of pants and a fishing jacket.'

'Niet!' said the Russian. 'It is not our business to outfit these people.' He said the prisoners' belongings, like watches and jewellery, that had been locked in the prison safe for all those years, could be handed back to them at 11.30 p.m. and their clothes given them at 11.55 p.m. They had five minutes to change.

Speer informed the directors he would stay in the Hotel Gerhus on his first night of freedom. Von Schirach chose the Berlin Hilton.

Before he departed, von Schirach – using a toilet paper wrapper – wrote Col. Bird a plea for Hess, who would be a lone prisoner in the huge jail.

Hess wishes to go to bed later and to return his eyeglasses later. He also wishes to rise earlier occasionally, to receive his glasses and to have his cell lighted if he does so. He wants to stay in the garden for a longer period and asks permission to read and write in the garden. He requests no censorship of books. He wishes to keep all his note-books. Wants letter paper one week in advance. Wants to own a watch or alarm clock.

Food: now and then southern German specialities; permission to ask for chocolates and sweets to be bought with money deposited by his family. Tea and powdered coffee at his disposal (for an extra cup between meals). Permission for his lawyer to see him if the lawyer wants to inform him about something; and permission to ask for and talk to his lawyer every three months. Permission to collect clippings from the daily papers. For hot summertime a double cell on the east side.

My suggestion: Permission to keep a little Dachel, a Bavarian dachshund, as a pet. Hess would have something to take care of, the dog would force him to take his exercise and keep him from always thinking of himself. (Talk to Hess about this – he would love to have the dog.)

Von Schirach had one more last-minute *gesuch* (request). 'Colonel, I have a request to make of you.' Patting his narrow cell bunk, he said: 'I have slept on this bed for 20 years. I have had many thoughts on this bed, read many hundreds of books; spent a great deal of my lifetime on it. I would like this bed crated up and sent to me so that I can make it into a couch and it will stay in our home and in my family forever. My grandchildren can look at it and say "this is where our grandfather slept for 20 years …"'

Col. Bird said a personal, warm farewell to his prisoner, Speer. 'Albert Speer was a man I admired a great deal. The way he lived, and took care of his health; working with the soil; planting flowers; making the garden beautiful. There was nothing but jungle before Speer got to it.

'Speer didn't have a lot of time for Hess. But he always watched out to make sure Hess didn't get a raw deal and [would] protest if Hess was being punished unjustly. He spoke for Hess when he was sick and went in and cleaned his cell. Speer always volunteered – cleaning and buffing the hallway; growing seeds for planting the next year.

'Speer was tall and gangly, there was no fat on him. His head was a bit larger than normal; his arms a bit longer. He would bow slightly at the hips to greet me, but not subserviently. He looked you straight in the eye, jumping off his bed to greet you. He had moles or warts on his face which were removed just prior to his release.

'Speer carried on his shoulders the weight of guilt for the crimes that he played a part in. He was one of the few at Nuremberg who stood up and admitted guilt. He had expected the death sentence.

'He said to me that he had become infatuated with Hitler; a Hitler with almost a hypnotic power. He had flown back on one of the last planes, to say goodbye to Hitler.

'Speer could get very angry. Once, during a British month, he protested against yet another meal of stew. "Stew! Stew! Only stew! Is the British Empire so poor that it can afford nothing but this stew? *Take it away!*"'

British warder W.R.Chisolm recorded another outburst by Speer over food, shortly before his release: 'I visited the cell section to see the food issued to the prisoners at 1130 hrs today. When Speer came to collect his food he was very rude and insulting to me in the presence of von Schirach, Hess and the US warder, Kyle. As usual, I said "good-day" to all prisoners. I could see Speer looked unpleasant and with a loud voice, he said: "What? Again goulash? Every time the same. Can't you do anything better? It is not good enough; you can't do this to me. I won't have it. Are you so poor you can't buy better food?" He said to me that if I could not do better he would complain to Mr Banfield [the British director]. I pointed out to him that "you have had fish, chicken, pork etc." But he said only once chicken and fish.

'He was bent on showing off in a very rude manner and did so. There were no complaints from Hess or von Schirach. Von Schirach was having a good laugh and indicated that he disagreed with Speer's actions.'

A few days later, Speer was punished for his display of temper. He would receive no books or newspapers for four days. He was allowed, however, to keep his Bible and his notebook.

Not only Speer, but Hess, too, could lose his temper. Soviet Chief Warder Kasakov reported that he had tried to get Hess up at the usual time, but he had refused, remaining in bed. 'So I was obliged to lift his bed-sheets, after which Hess got up rushily [sic], with his fists clenched and crying and gesticulating in my direction, showing great signs of discontent and threatening me. I ask the directors to take against Hess measures of most severe punishment.'

Hess was placed in a special cell for five successive days, from 8 a.m. – 5 p.m., deprived of books and newspapers.

CHAPTER 14

THEY'RE OUT!

O n the night of the prisoners' release, with scores of media and
inquisitive Berliners crowding the streets outside the prison, Bird
and a warder walked quietly past Hess's cell. 'We thought he was
sleeping. I asked him if he had heard anything going on in the hallway.'

This was now the lone prisoner's daily Spandau schedule:

Hess is awakened each day by a warder tapping on his small window. If it
is winter and dark, he can switch his light on. In summer the sun will be
shining through his two cell windows in his new cell, previously occupied
by Funk and then von Schirach. Wearing striped blue-and-white pyjamas,
he reaches down with his feet to the small stand under his bunk and steps
into his slippers.

He puts on his hospital bathrobe, takes a white towel from a shelf and
shuffles through the unlocked cell door, past a seated warder, to the toilet.
He then takes 28 steps to the bathroom where he washes and shaves with
his Braun electric razor.

At 7.45 AM his breakfast is brought to his cell on the rubber-wheeled
food trolley. He has egg, toast, fruit and coffee. He has his coffee without
sugar (it makes him 'fat') and with a little milk.

From 8.30 AM he takes socks, underwear to wash in the washroom.

Some time after the others had gone, Hess said to Col. Bird: 'You know, the worst thing about being in prison is the loneliness. Not being able to talk to someone. To tell someone about joys, fears, wants; someone who is interested. All day long I am surrounded by people, but I really have no-one to talk to. I can't converse with the warders. They are good people, but their ability to converse along the lines I would like, is limited. Or at least it limits them.'

But Hess had his birds. Every day, twice a day, birds awaited Hess in the garden. Crows, pigeons and song birds flew in waiting for the old man, with his paper bags full of crumbs from the kitchen, to make his solitary walks in the morning and afternoon.

He was still having discomfort with an upper denture. His top teeth had been removed under local anaesthetic, an impression taken and a denture constructed; but it did not seem to fit. He still had a lower right molar and four lower median incisors. When dentists decided a root canal of a tooth had to be removed, Hess asked that the whole tooth be extracted. 'If there is a possibility that one can make a cap, that is alright. But we will have to be careful about that, because if the root is gone and the nerve too, there could be an abscess and I would never feel it.'

He was annoyed (he told Ilse in a letter) with a reported interview with Speer, in which Speer was quoted as saying Hess had gone through a 'specially terrible' time for three days when Speer and von Schirach had been released. 'Not true,' wrote Hess, 'there can be no talk of terrible days. I was as even-tempered as ever.'

He had another visit from his lawyer, Seidl, and there was an uncomfortable atmosphere between the two. Was it true, Hess asked his old defender, that Seidl had given information to the press that made it appear that Hess was mentally unstable? If so, he demanded that it be corrected. He was absolutely positive he had never had such trouble.

Seidl denied it. He said he had had long talks with Speer and von Schirach following their release and they had both assured him that Hess was mentally stable. Hess accepted what Seidl had said, but nevertheless asked him to issue a statement at the next opportunity attesting to his mental stability. But healthwise he was not in good shape, he said; he still had heart, stomach and bladder problems. Seidl departed, giving Hess his assurance that he would never work on his old client's release based on Hess being mentally unstable.

Prison doctors were recommending alterations to Hess's daily schedule. Hess was now in his seventy-third year. He now found it difficult to wake at 6 a.m. and remained listless and irritable throughout the day. It was better that he should be allowed to remain asleep until 6.45 a.m., with breakfast time and bed-making postponed until later. His doctors pointed out that he was no longer physically able to do heavy work, like polishing floors or laundering sheets; however, he was capable of doing light work, like dusting, bed-making and washing his underclothes. It was also recommended that the stock of dangerous drugs kept in the safe in the old chief warder's office be destroyed because they had not been used for many years.

CHAPTER 15

I AM HARMLESS NOW

I t was no secret that the Allied powers were in favour of Hess's release to his family, but the Russians were obstinate in their refusal. Hess said to Bird: 'I cannot understand for the life of me why the Russians will not agree to my release. They must know I only have a short time to live. I'm an old man and I'm perfectly harmless in my state; or would be, in any political light. They must harbour some hatred towards me. They may let me out, I suppose, when they realise I am very sick and only have a short time to live. Then the world will be screaming for my release.'

He went on: 'I told General Franklin, the former US City Commandant, that other political prisoners, condemned to life imprisonment, and even those condemned to die, have long since been released from prisons. Look at Funk and von Neurath. But I have to stay on. And it is not right.'

Bird listened politely as Hess, turning to his right side on the bunk, supported by his right elbow, made his statement. 'By the way, Colonel, I have dropped the idea of your kidnapping me. You will recall I asked you that when I first went into hospital. I was weak and feverish and one says funny things like that … I realise now it was fantasy.'

He would have been upset, said Bird, if he had heard a conversation around the directors' dining table regarding the arrangements to be made when Hess eventually passed away. British director Ralph Banfield pointed

134

to a valuable antique cabinet in the dining room and wondered what would happen to it if Hess died or was released.

'Release?' said the Russian. 'Life in prison really means life.'

Said Bird: 'The flying suit is more important. Make it so the man in the [director's] chair at the time gets the flying suit.'

The Russian said: 'No. Let's burn the flying suit.'

'Burn it?' exclaimed Bird. 'D'you know what that suit is worth? It's an antique.'

'You're the businessman,' said the Russian, 'what is it worth?'

Bird: 'Fifty thousand dollars. And when the time comes it should be given back to the British. They brought it here and they should get it back.'

Gene Bird made a point of visiting Hess daily, repeatedly asking him about the past, about Hitler and his flight. He secretly took Polaroid shots of him in his cell and in the garden feeding his birds; lying on his bunk; watching television for the first time on a set the Soviets had reluctantly allowed him to have in the hospital and which had been brought with him to the prison. And reading the pages of this draft manuscript.

Bird had prepared a legal contract which said (in part):

I Eugene Bird, Lt. Col. (U.S.A. Rtd) state that I have commissioned Mr Desmond Zwar of 65 Cadogan Gardens, London, SW3, to write a book with me concerning Spandau Allied Prison, and in particular, Rudolf Hess, the only remaining prisoner. In my position as US Prison Governor, I have seen and talked to Rudolf Hess on almost a daily basis for nearly ten years. All information furnished Mr Desmond Zwar for the subject book has been taken from authenticated, written material or first-person conversations between Hess and myself. Much of this information has never appeared in print before.

Mr Hess has full knowledge of the pending book, has given me his wholehearted approval to it and is in the process of furnishing me information and material for the book, to the best of his ability and memory to date. I have read the manuscript (of which I have an up-to-date copy) and am in full accord and agreement with the way it has been written.

Most evenings Gene Bird and I sat over his tape-recorder – on which he had recorded his Hess conversations.

He said on tape that Hess methodically started each day with the same ritual at 6.45 a.m; wearing blue-and-white striped pyjamas he would place his hands on his hips and do squatting and jumping exercises, breathing deeply and stretching. Removing his dentures on the way to the bathroom he would clean them; then shave, using a Braun electric razor, running it across his gaunt cheeks and over the dark stubble on his wide upper lip. He would then blow out the razor and replace it in his locker. Then he would strip to the waist and wash.

One morning, Gene Bird had found the former deputy Führer in a reflective mood, for the first time happy to discuss his relationship with Adolf Hitler. 'There was,' Hess told Bird, 'only a certain point of familiarity you could reach with Hitler, you know. Beyond that point you could not go. There were times I felt close to him, but they were very seldom. He never revealed much warmth. He kept himself aloof. I think he felt superior to the people around him and to the common folk. His inner sense of superiority probably made him the way he was.

'I, for instance, never used the familiar "Du" when addressing him. I always said "Sie". We were always on "Sie" terms. Even in the early days, and during the war when we worked closely together. As Speer said [Albert Speer gave an interview to *Playboy* magazine in June 1971, and Bird had taken it in to show Hess], there were only four people who used "Du" to Hitler – Rhoem, Julius Streicher, Christian Weber and Hermann Esser. And of course Eva Braun. Actually it was unwise to become too familiar – look what happened to Rhoem!

'Speer gained the admiration of the Führer for his ability and his genius; and perhaps because of his ability to meet deadlines and even be ahead of them. Hitler was an amateur architect and so he felt he and Speer spoke the same language.'

Col. Bird: 'Do you think Hitler is dead?'

'Oh, of course,' said Hess as the tape revolved. 'There were stories that he escaped to South America but they were not true. He would never have run away. So far as I am concerned, he definitely committed suicide. It would have been entirely against his nature to escape from Germany and go and live somewhere else. He, too, was dedicated and had his ideals. When he realised that all was lost, that the war would soon be over, I believe he would have certainly decided to take his own life. He most certainly would not have wanted to turn himself over to the Russians – that would have been worse than death.

'Like most of us,' Hess told Bird, 'Hitler feared death. He worried a lot about being assassinated, as there had been several attempts on his life. I have read recently that the Russians have absolute proof of finding his remains outside the bunker; they even have a photograph. I believe them.

'I was not there, of course, in the final stages, but I believe he could have arranged for many people to have the means of suicide; the Goebbels family for instance, and Himmler, and of course Goering who committed suicide at Nuremberg. I do believe that Martin Bormann fled in the last hours. Possibly to South America. It would be in keeping with his nature.'

'You didn't care for Bormann?'

'I was never jealous of him, or Goering; that is what people keep on saying or writing. I was never jealous of any person.'

'Did you know that Hitler's real name in Austria was Schicklgruber?'

Both men laughed. 'Yes, well you could hardly call out "Heil! Schicklgruber!" That was certainly one of the reasons he changed it,' said Hess.

Bird later told me: 'Glancing about his cell I noticed open on the bed-table the scientific dictionary which had been bought for 106 DM from prison funds at Hess's request. It gave an explanation of space terminology, in English and German. Hess, in his thirst for space information, was reading daily long and complicated details of the moon landings and probes. Hanging from the walls and suspended from the cell ceiling were photographs of the moon's surface sent by NASA from Houston. He had brochures and timetables, interviews with the cosmonauts and piles of cuttings from his newspapers. Hess asked me if I had sent on to NASA his suggestions for a revolving exercise platform. I said I had. "You know they have been most kind to me," he said. "Would it not be a good idea to send off a signed photograph of me? I would autograph it and date it and they could have it as a token of my thanks." He had already autographed another photograph for an official of the Archives – a stiff, official Nazi portrait in full uniform. I tried to imagine Speer or von Schirach doing the same and could not. Hess was still a vain man.

'He picked up a newspaper lying on his bed. "I wanted to show you this. Here is a doctor who exactly agrees with what I said about cosmonauts needing exercise. He states that if you exercise daily to the point where your heart-beat is increasing rapidly over a three-minute period, you are strengthening your heart muscles. It is just what I was saying. If they build a platform as I suggest it would very much improve their blood circulation."

'I asked him if his clock still kept good time. "Excellent. Excellent." He had tampered with it for days, with a special tool made by the prison hand-yman, so it lost less than six seconds in 24 hours.

'NASA had sent him a minute-by-minute timetable of space activity for Apollo 15 and Hess wished to follow what was going on. The clock had an alarm and he had it set for the various direct broadcasts coming from Houston. A warder had "unofficially" brought in a small transistor radio for the occasion and we pretended it wasn't there during the Apollo mission.

'Hess's bed had not been slept in the night before. Now the Berlin weather had become so hot he had asked if he could sleep on the cooler side of the cell-block. He had been given access to Cell 13 and his old bed from Cell 23 had been brought in – much to the annoyance of the fat French warder Barcanan, who used it to catch up on his sleep at quiet times during the night. Barcanan snored louder than any man I have heard, the noise penetrating through the cell walls and out through the cell-block into the yard. Hess requested that when he was on duty outside his cell, his warder's table and chair be moved as far away as possible so that the prisoner himself could get some sleep. Every night he pushed his wax ear-plugs deep into his ears, but even they were not enough to keep out Barcanan's trumpeting. "I even have to wake the fellow in the morning," Hess grumbled.

'He then began to busy himself in the cell, preparing it for an official visit by Major-General Cobb, the US Commandant in Berlin, later in the day. When the general arrived, Hess was smartly dressed in a new light-blue sports jacket which had replaced his frayed denims. He was polite and chatty, as he had been with me a few hours before. He and the general had a twenty-minute discussion on food, Hess's health, the Olympic Games and the idea that a Russian and an American cosmonaut might one day fly together in space. When I told General Cobb that Hess's flying suit and Luftwaffe uniform in which he had flown to Scotland were nearby in the storeroom the old man chuckled with pride. When the general said he saw no reason why the prisoner should not have access to a small television set to watch the next space shot, Hess nodded excitedly. "That would be excellent!" – "And perhaps you might like to see the Munich Olympics on it," said General Cobb. Hess agreed. He had watched the 1936 Berlin Olympics, he said. He did not mention that it had been under different circumstances.

'General Cobb departed and soon after, a glossy volume from the United States Information Service called *Das Grosse Projekt* – the story of American space exploration – arrived for Hess with the general's compliments. "That was very good of him," said No. 7. "Do you think I could send him a photograph of me signed, with a letter of thanks?" I told him the letter would be enough.

'During the visit nothing had been mentioned of the Four-Power talks on Berlin. They had just reached agreement and many were wondering whether they had discussed Hess. He discounted the idea. "No, I don't believe they would have discussed me."'

'If you had your time over again, Mr Hess,' asked Bird one day, 'would you again serve a man like Hitler?' Hess, in crumpled denims and his shirt hanging out under his braces, looked at him. 'What do you mean? Yes. I believe I would travel the same route; end up here again in Spandau prison. I wanted to give Germany back its old pride and its old fame.'

'And you would again serve under a man like Hitler?' He looked at his questioner over his spectacles.

'I would not have wanted to miss the opportunity of serving Adolf Hitler as his deputy. I was a dedicated man. A dedicated man who meant to do good.'

Bird asked him why he became involved in the Nazi movement in the first place.

'To bring back Germany's old pride and old fame. This is what I had in mind when I became active in politics as a young man in 1923. I became involved in the direction the entire flow was leading.'

And his decision to fly to Scotland? 'I knew there was only one way out. And that was certainly not to fight against England. We could not win a two-front war.'

'Tell me a single young person,' Hess demanded, 'who is in world politics today, who is not interested in bettering the situation as it stands. Even though I did not get permission from the Führer [to fly] I knew that what I had to say would have had his approval. He did not want to fight against England.'

Sitting in Cell 23 he set out his own version of his flight – and his fate. He wrote on 20 September 1971:

> In many ways we realise – also through Churchill – that Rudolf Hess flew to England [sic] out of his own decision – not through orders from Hitler.
>
> He risked his life with the intention to initiate the fastest way of ending the war through peace – Communication.
>
> He believed in helping the people concerned, but furthermore, to help the whole of humanity through his action. It is therefore not understandable that the British took him to Nürnberg to hand him over to the courts. On top of this they agreed, after the Process, to bring him to Spandau. With this decision he was practically handed over to the Russians.
>
> They were given the right of veto to either incarcerate him indefinitely or allow his freedom. Also Sir Winston was compliant in this decision.
>
> Consequently, especially Great Britain will appear to publicly press for Hess's final release.
>
> Handed to Col. Bird.

Hess was now co-operating with Col. Bird and me, answering the typed questions I sent for him to read. Was his flight actually to save humanity or was Goering pushing him out of power? Did Hitler have any idea that he would fly? Beside my question 'You said the Führer did not want to defeat England – that he wanted an understanding with Britain?' he scrawled *richtig* (correct!) and initialled it.

Then I asked: Do you remember the letter you wrote to the Duke of Hamilton – and what you wrote? You must remember what you put in your letter to Hitler that was to be delivered by Pintsch after you set off?

Hess replied in writing: 'I cannot remember the letter to the Duke of Hamilton. Naturally I explained myself in the letter to Hitler regarding my intentions for my flight to England. But I cannot recall the details or wording of this letter.'

CHAPTER 16

DEAR DOG ...

I t was now time to take my London literary agent, George Greenfield, of John Farquharson Ltd, one of the longest-established literary agencies in Britain, into our confidence. We were sitting on a literary time bomb of international significance; should Hess suddenly die − or worse − if Bird and I were found out, we would need to know the worth of what we already had and what to do with it. In great confidence I went to the old-fashioned suite of offices at 15 Red Lion Square in London to see Greenfield, whose office was lined with photographs of his famous clients: Enid Blyton, Sir Chris Bonnington, David Niven, Jeffrey Archer − and, ironically, Dame Laura Knight, who had set me on the Nazi trail in the first place.

After my visit he wrote to me: 'The more I think of this project the more excited I become about it. It has been a great temptation to drop even the merest hint to various visiting American publishers ... but I promise my lips are firmly sealed!'

Conservative, cigar-smoking and renowned as absolutely trustworthy, George Greenfield was to 'nurse' myself and Gene Bird for five long years as the risks went on; through snooping by the Foreign Office and the US State Department, to nasty ultimatums from German lawyers. Risks of the project being 'blown' abounded. Why was the US director so often seen chatting to Hess in the garden?, the suspicious Soviet director had asked a warder. What was he doing in Hess's cell? When it was necessary for Greenfield to communicate with Col. Bird, an elaborate false name and 'drop address' were arranged. Bird was 'Herr Nelte'. The Hess book was a Mercedes 600, for which good offers were anticipated.

When I had come back from my first visit to Berlin and talked to George Greenfield about the colonel, George wrote to him:

> We have recently celebrated our fiftieth anniversary as an agency. During this time we have handled many major literary projects. Such 'epics' as the first ever crossing of Antarctica and the solo voyage around the world of Sir Francis Chichester. Thus, when I say that in my opinion the story you have to tell ranks in significance, I am not speaking ill-advisedly.
>
> It will be a great historic document.

As our collaboration with Hess gathered pace, and the fear of discovery grew, Greenfield and Bird began talking and writing in code to each other. Bird signed himself 'Bazi' (which was the name of his dog).

George told me that one Sunday Gene had called him from the garden 'to ask what the weather is like over there'. 'And we had a rather inane conversation about "the sun beginning to shine brightly" which would have been obvious even to the most stupid CIA man who might have tapped the line!'

Col. Bird, armed with his Polaroid camera, was enthusiastically (and dangerously) shooting Hess in his cell, in the garden; photographing him carefully examining the flying suit he had worn when he parachuted into Scotland, showing him reading the draft chapters of my manuscript and editing it.

By the end of August 1970, Hess's health was improving. He greeted Gene Bird from his seat in the garden and agreed to answer further questions I had sent in to him, which the colonel gave him to read.

DZ: 'Mr Hess, how many books do you read in a week?'

Hess: 'That depends, of course, on the type of book and the contents of the book. I have read one book in a week and I have also taken several weeks to read one book. I am an avid reader; I read all the time.'

DZ: 'What sort of books most interest you? Scientific or historical?'

Hess: 'I like reading [both]. I also like to read about the economy. I like history from the Middle Ages to modern history. I am reading at the moment articles and books on the moon. I am interested in the moon's surface and the problem of the craters. I am at the moment reading *The Face of the Moon* by Baldwin.'

DZ: 'Which writer has given you the most guidance in your life?'

Hess: 'Without a doubt the writer who has given me the most guidance is Shopenhauer.'

DZ: 'What sort of guidance?'

Hess: 'He strengthened my inner conviction that man is guided by Fate. Therefore I am sure that one day I shall be set free!' (He had Col. Bird write and rewrite this answer to make sure it was correct.) 'Everything that comes – that happens in our life – is because of Fate. There are times when we have the power to guide our fate; by doing things ourselves that will determine that fate. But at the end of it all, Man is guided by Fate.'

At the end of this talk he told Bird he wanted to add something about Shopenhauer. He was, he said, most impressed by what Shopenhauer had written about the strength of Nature – 'which from all sides manifests itself and which lets the stars rotate and circle after external laws which were never changing; which allows all kinds of living matter to develop after a pattern. Yet there is a will that is so strong,' said Hess, 'that it can influence both body and spirit.' He had shown by 'self-experimentation' that this was true.

'Without this will,' he said into Bird's tape-recorder, 'I would not have been able to hold through the past many years.'

Bird warned me at the end of the tape he sent me: 'Don't mention spiders and that I kill them. He is against killing!'

The old man had a comment – about Saxons. He asked Bird: 'Is your wife Saxon?'

'No, she is a Berliner.'

'Well,' said Hess, 'as far as I know the Saxons are not popular with the other parts of Germany. Maybe it's because of the dialect they have. In my younger days, I could see the most beautiful girl under the moon; but when she opened her mouth and spoke Saxon dialect, everything was over from that moment on. That doesn't mean they're not good people. I just couldn't stand the dialect.' (Hess wasn't to know that my great-grandfather was a Saxon!)

He was in a chatty mood and Bird asked him whether he had in fact crashed an aircraft during the First World War. 'No. Not true. I have flown many planes. To me, flying is like a fish swimming in the water.'

'It's the 10th of May, 1971, 30 years to the day since Hess flew from Germany on his mission. It was his 77th birthday recently and I got him a knife and fork to use. It's the first time he has been allowed to handle a knife in 30 years. Can you imagine that!

'I had lunch at Spandau and then went into the garden with your questions to see Hess. It was a beautiful day; the sun was shining and it was hot. When I told him what anniversary it was, Hess said: "Oh! I had even forgotten about it."

'I also took him a sound tape of the BBC programme commemorating the flight, and played the first 20 minutes to him. We were sitting under a tree planted by Doenitz. I also had with me a pair of sandals he wanted very much – I'd had to change them three times and now had a 44 size. They are a health sandal.'

Hess was wearing a grey denim suit, blue socks cut off at the ankles, light blue summer shoes with perforations, and he had a white silk scarf around his neck. He looked healthy. He had his feet stretched out resting on the bench in front of him. The colonel's Sony tape-recorder lay on a briefcase between Hess and his questioner.

'Mr Hess, you told me before that nobody knew about your plans to make the flight. But there were people who said they knew about it?'

'What do you mean?'

'Hamilton's [the Duke of Hamilton's] book brings out letters you had exchanged with Albrecht and Karl Haushofer. And it was talked over at great length regarding a possible understanding with the United Kingdom. You cannot say you came about this idea all by yourself.'

'Listen, Colonel. I said that I flew on my own – that nobody *knew* I was going to fly. I took this on my own shoulders to do. Of course I talked about the plan that I had in mind prior to flying. And I was in touch with Dr Albrecht Haushofer and Professor Karl Haushofer. I have never denied it; you have never asked me as much. I flew on my own and I took it on myself to fly. My mission was a great mission – a mission for humanity. It was a mission to end the war and bring about an understanding with England. To stop the bloodshed and the suffering. Little did I know that Churchill did not have the power to stop the rolling stone. It was impossible. I went too late. As a result, my mission was a failure. But it was a great mission, I repeat.'

'Did you really have high hopes that you could bring about a settlement with the British? Peace?'

'If I had not high hopes, I obviously would not have flown to England. You have the letters that show the attempt to talk to the Duke of Hamilton. I would like to see the letters and perhaps I can comment after I see them.'

'Did Hitler know about your flight – you preparation for the flight?'

'Look, Hitler never wanted to fight against England. I knew that from the early days in France. Hitler actually had great respect for the English people.'

'In view of the book by Hamilton that has come out, with the exchanges of letters between you and Haushofer, you have simply got to state more clearly whether Hitler did know. Let me ask you again: did Hitler know about your (intended) flight to England?'

'Well, does the book say he knew?'

'Please answer the questions and I want you to be as fair to me as you possibly can. Our book has to be true and factual, otherwise it will be a laughing stock. Did Hitler know?'

Bird spoke again for the benefit of the tape: 'He stammered and looked away. He said: "Colonel Bird, I don't know. I can't remember."'

Bird pushed Hess for an answer: 'This is ridiculous! You must know!'

Then Hess said: 'At this point I really have nothing further to say; except to say that I didn't realise then, that thirty years later I would be sitting in this garden under this tree listening to a BBC documentary on my flight to England. Thirty years ago was a much more exciting time for me than it is on this day.'

As Bird pressed the 'play' button and the English voice came on, Hess's chin jutted out, his brow was furrowed and he gazed at his hands which were folded over his stomach. He asked several times for the tape to be stopped and re-played, shaking his head. He laughed out loud when a Captain McDonald said he had interviewed Hess 'and he told me his name was Alfred Horn'.

'Ah,' chuckled Hess, 'he knew who I was.'

He told Bird he often thought about 'injustice', wondering about what would have happened if his peace overtures had succeeded: 'Would I have got the Nobel Prize, like Willi Brandt, instead of now being in prison?'

Reading the latest chapters I had written, Hess was annoyed that I had also recorded his tantrums and his childlike hoarding of food scraps (which he alleged would be shown to contain poison). He grumpily scrawled 'NEIN!' beside the offending paragraphs.

It was already ten minutes past the time Hess had been allowed to sit in the garden, and director and prisoner got up to make their way back into the prison. Bird asked about the authorship of the book *Mein Kampf*. 'You said before that you did not write part of the book with Hitler. But it has been written in black and white that you took down the dictated words from Hitler. That being a studied man, you passed on many of your ideas in regard to *lebensraum* (living room for the German people) and you put it into the mind of Hitler? And they appeared in *Mein Kampf*?'

'Yes. That's right. But many of the ideas that were passed on to Hitler for his book came from Professor Karl Haushofer. But they were misconstrued by Hitler. He was not a studied man. He took the ideas from the great professor, but he changed them in his own mind to fit in with his purposes.'

'The "loss of memory" you had in England. Were you feigning this or was it the truth?'

Hess again stuttered and stammered as he replied; they were on their way inside the prison. 'Colonel Bird, anyone who has been in prison as long as I have, and at my age, of course my memory is bad. Part of it *was* put on, but I do have trouble with my memory.'

'Goering was in a more powerful position than you. Were you being overshadowed by him?'

'No. No. No. This was not the case. Not true at all.' Then he added: 'Hitler, you know, had great respect for the British people, the British Empire and British culture and the civilisation that Britain had brought into the world ...'

Back in the cell now, Bird asked him: 'Did you know about the pending attack on Russia? Hamilton claims that you did and that you were on the central planning committee and that you must have known?'

He evaded the question, Bird said. 'My suspicion is that he knew. His jaw dropped down and his face got longer and even changed colour, becoming pale; his eyes seemed more sunken than before, and I felt it was time to stop.'

Now Hess sat down on his bunk in Cell 23, and Bird decided to try once more: 'You must have known something about Hitler's intention to attack the Soviet Union before you took off. The Russians have always thought so.'

'I told you the last time [it was discussed] that I would think about it. I did think; and I wrote down the answer to your question. You may use what I wrote in your book if you wish.'

Hess rummaged amongst books in his makeshift bookcase and took out a piece of paper on which he had written in ink: 'Before I flew to Scotland I did not know of Hitler's intention to attack Russia. I did know, however, that he was no friend of the Soviet Union. Hitler did not know of my flight prior to me making it.'

Bird later told me: 'That was, he said, all he wished to tell me about the matter. In other words, would I kindly drop the subject?'

Hess said finally: 'In reality I haven't told you much. And that bothers me. You must understand that I am searching my memory as much as I possibly can. I want your book to be a good book and I want it to go down in history as being the factual story about me.'

The old man again showed he could get angry. He wrote a complaint to the Spandau directors about what he called 'his working hours'.

I have put up with this theatre for the last 28 years as a prisoner in this prison. I am not going to continue this theatre for the 29th year. I consider it beneath my dignity to work in the garden just to get two hours more exercise. I don't care if it is just pulling out some weeds or raking some leaves, but I can't stand in one place.

When he was in hospital he had complained to Col. Bird: 'Look at this letter from my wife on 25th February. It has been censored again; whole paragraphs cut out of it. Why can't they – if she has written too many words – subtract the words from her next letter? Or ask her not to write so much? I understand there are hundreds of letters which come to me. I never see them. They are destroyed. I think they should be saved for me so I can at least write and thank these good people if and when I am ever released. They are addressed to me and should be mine. Last night the Russian warder came in and saw my wife's flowers behind the bars of the windows. He took them away because "they were against regulations". Why can't I have the flowers?'

CHAPTER 17

SMUGGLERS AND SPOOKS

It was getting close to the time for me to leave Berlin. We had accumulated many hours of interviews with Hess on recording tape. And because Berlin was surrounded by Soviet-controlled East Germany, the smuggling operation of transcripts, photographs and documents had to be by air. There was no way I could drive my VW car from Berlin, through the Russian-occupied sector to Hanover on the Allied-occupied border, with Hess's tapes and writings. It was decided that Delphine would be the courier and I would drive through the East 'clean'.

As departure time drew near my fears grew. Delphine would carry the Hess papers, photographs and tapes in an attaché case on her knees on the plane; allowing it to be checked in as hold luggage was out of the question. What if the case was examined before she took off? And what was going to happen to me en route to the West by road, when every KGB man worth his salt would have been aware of my British-registered, identifiable car parked outside the US director's residence day after day?

I set off at 4 a.m. in pitch darkness, three hours before Colonel Bird was to drive Delphine and the papers to Tempelhof. It was windy and bitterly cold. Worse, the roads had turned to ice and I was driving before the snow-ploughs had moved in to clear it. Between Berlin and Magdeburg the wind had reached gale force and my car was being pushed from one side of the road to the other as though I was driving on a skating rink. My stomach was empty and churning. I feared the worst as I headed for the Eastern sector border. Would the Russians and East Germans have decided that was where I was to be grabbed?

I reached the border guard gate and it was snowing heavily. I drove through to the end of a queue of cars, slowly inching forward as armed guards slid mirrors beneath them looking for people trying to smuggle themselves out of the Soviet sector to freedom. Car boots were opened, even back seats torn out for inspection. Then they got to me. A gruff character in a long greatcoat came up to my driving window and pointed left. '*Aus!*' he said. '*Aus!*' He was motioning for me to leave the queue and park by a large shed.

I had been caught!

I parked and shakily got out. '*Nicht verstanden*,' I tried. 'I don't understand'.

'*Kommen-sie*,' he said. I had to follow him inside. There was a bespectacled official behind a window. Hands trembling, I offered him my passport, showing him my visa. He glanced at it and stuck out his chin. '*Nein!*' Then he spoke in English. 'Your papers are in order. Your car was in the wrong queue. You were in the US Army vehicle queue. Drive to the right one.' I had merely driven behind the last car, not noticing its distinctive coloured number plate that designated it as US Forces.

A guard shoved his mirror under my VW, stood up and grinned at me. '*Ist gut*,' he said, and waved me through to the American checkpoint.

Delphine was waiting for me at the airport, rugged up and smiling; Hess documents and pictures intact. We went to the restaurant, opened a bottle of French champagne and hugged each other.

We had decided to move back to Australia, to the north Queensland city of Cairns, a laid-back tropical paradise. The 10,000-mile distance from Europe now meant a longer delay between my weekly questions being read to Hess and my getting his replies. And because the cassette tapes Gene Bird was airmailing me had to go through Her Majesty's Customs before they reached the Cairns post office a mile away, I was always concerned that somebody would play one of them – and our four-year secret would be blown.

But so far it had not happened. My Q&A with the deputy Führer was proceeding undisturbed by officialdom.

On one particular tape Hess greeted Col. Bird as he was ushered into his cell. 'I have been reading a newspaper article about German youth,' Hess said. 'You know, with all the criticisms levelled at von Schirach and his Hitler Jugend, it is forgotten that he did a fantastic thing with Germany's young. He kept them busy, he kept them out of trouble. He had a health programme and health camps for them to enjoy. In those years we did not have to concern ourselves with the worry of youths taking drugs, getting involved in crime, and sexual permissiveness. We did not have the burning of national flags and draft cards. We had a healthy young with healthy minds, all pulling together under one flag to build a nation. That is what we need today,' he said, waving a finger, 'we need to get them back on the right track.'

'But surely,' said Col. Bird, 'you were doing all this with youth for a different purpose. You were building a super-race for war, for conquests; to make Germany the strongest nation in Europe. Today youth is rebelling because we made a mess of their world.'

'Maybe, but they won't make a better world with drugs,' Hess growled.

Bird had brought with him a further batch of pages from the manuscript of our book, which Hess was assiduously going through. Bird had allowed him to keep forty-four pages of it overnight in his cell. Hess turned to page 30 of the manuscript and said: 'I want to talk to you about this paragraph on Barbarossa. You had written that Hitler was worried – when I flew – "that Hess might reveal his Führer's plan to attack Russia. Hess was one of the few who knew of the planned attack to take place six weeks later. And Hitler was horrified that Hess might betray it." Then you drew a line through it all. Why did you do that?'

'Because when I wrote it,' said Bird, 'I believed it to be the truth. But after talking to you to check it out you emphatically denied it. I crossed the whole paragraph out. If you say something I have put in that manuscript is not true – not as it happened at the time – then it will not go into our book.'

Hess looked at Bird steadily. 'Colonel, I want you to leave that paragraph in, just the way you had it.' Bird asked him to repeat what he said. 'I want that paragraph to stand,' said Hess.

'Do you realize what you are saying? You are admitting to me that you knew about Barbarossa before you flew off to Scotland.'

'Colonel – I am asking you to leave what you had originally written.'

'Then you did know about Barbarossa?'

'Yes, I did.' And stepping into his down-at-heel carpet slippers he shuffled off to the bathroom.

Bird saw him again the next day, hardly daring to broach the subject again. 'I made that alteration in the manuscript,' he said casually.

'Yes,' Hess replied. 'Yes, I did know. We can discuss it fully at a later date.'

'Then tell me about it. You have just made an extremely important statement – important to History.'

'Not now,' said Hess. 'It suffices to say that I wish you to record that fact as you originally recorded it before you struck it out.'

On Bird's next visit, Hess had just climbed the three steps into his former hospital bed when the director entered his cell. He squatted on the horsehair wedge, leaning against four pillows. The two shook hands and Hess began talking about his recent session with the doctor.

Our manuscript was, by now, a thick book and it had been secretly shown by our literary agent, under an agreed contract of confidentiality, to several leading publishers.

But at the same time (without informing me), Gene Bird had his mind on another outlet for the Hess prison saga: television. In great confidentiality he flew to London in November 1972, and was introduced to a director of Independent Television News and given a crash course in operating a new, hand-held, sound-on-film camera. He smuggled it into Spandau and interviewed Hess in the garden and in his cell for twenty-nine minutes, making a documentary worth many thousands of dollars. Bird then flew back to ITN in London with camera and film.

On his return to Tempelhof airport, Berlin, Bird discovered his suitcase was missing. Assured it would turn up he drove to his home to find guards surrounding the house. As he stepped from his Mercedes, he was told he had been placed under house arrest. This time we *had* been found out.

Gene Bird was flown to Washington from where he phoned me in distress, obviously fearful for his future. Gone was the boyish excitement in his voice; he was stammering. He said he had been under intense questioning and then ordered to sign the US Secrets Act which he had never had to sign previously – effective retrospectively. His own massive file of papers and photographs had been seized from his house in Fischottersteig and he had been formally sacked as a Spandau director.

He pleaded with me on the phone: 'Send everything you have, the manuscript of our book, the photographs, everything, to the State Department. We are both in bad trouble. The Soviets have gone crazy about the way this thing happened under their noses. If you don't do so *they* will lean on you from your nearest capital city.'

Assuming his call was either supervised or tapped, I refused. 'I am not a US citizen, Colonel, and the State Department has no rights to anything I have written,' I stammered. 'I will write the book under my own name and will not even mention you.' And put down the phone. I did not have to think too hard about who *they* were.

Then an alarming thing happened in Cairns, Queensland – many thousands of miles from the US State Department. I was publishing a weekly free newspaper in order to provide us with a living while I was writing the Hess saga. Around 11 a.m. Delphine phoned me at my office. She said she had walked into our large, dingy cellar under the house – situated on a mountainside at Stratford, a fairly remote spot, 8 km from the city – and she had found two men there; one, wearing mirror sunglasses, spoke to her in an American accent.

They were a few feet away from a wall where I kept all the Hess word-tapes, his handwritten and typewritten manifesto and diaries, and all Bird's Polaroid photographs – hidden in a row of hollow cement wall-bricks that I had covered over with mortar. Delphine bravely asked the men what they were doing there. 'They said they were looking for our pool,' she told me. 'They wanted to give us a quote to put a pebble substance on the rough pool surrounds.' One thrust a business card at my wife. She firmly asked them to leave.

When I raced home she was still shaken from the experience. I immediately called the Cairns distributor for the product on the business card and asked if the two men really worked as representatives for him.

'Yes,' he said. 'Nice blokes. They've only been with me for a few days. Very enthusiastic. They went and got their own business cards printed.'

I remembered what Gene Bird had said: *they* would be sent from the nearest capital city. He could only have meant the CIA. The next Sunday morning I telephoned the US consul at his home in Brisbane and said I was the co-author of a book on Hess with Colonel Eugene Bird and that I had recently had a visit from two men I believed were Secret Service operatives. He said he knew nothing about it.

I said: 'Of course. But please write this down. Please tell the people in Washington that I am going ahead with publishing the book, but that it will not even mention Gene Bird. It will come out under my own name.'

At this time – unbeknown to either Gene Bird or me – 'spooks' from the US State Department and the British Foreign Office were also at work. They had long ago discovered Col. Bird was collaborating with Rudolf Hess and me.

Thirty years later, the details of their sleuthing were made public – by a Russian. It was New Year's Day 2003, and I had a strange phone message. Would I please call Mr Serge Morozov of Russian Channel Six TV in London? Urgently! It was about Rudolf Hess.

I called Serge Morozov, and he told me: 'As of today all the files of 30 years ago have been declassified under the 30-year rule, and there are some sensational documents released by the Public Record Office regarding the book you and Colonel Bird wrote about the imprisonment of Rudolf Hess. The papers reveal the panic the American and British governments experienced when they were told that Hess was collaborating with you and Mr Bird.' Serge told me he was preparing a television programme on the declassified papers and wished to interview me on tape – and Colonel Bird, if he could find him. He would email me the documents.

That night they slowly appeared on my computer screen, in no sequential order.

CONFIDENTIAL. British Embassy, Washington. 16 May 1972 to FCO [Foreign Office in London].
Bird is now in Florida ... (he had been arrested in Berlin and flown to the US) there is some doubt whether he can be prosecuted, but the general feeling is that it is problematical and would be counterproductive, in that

it would produce unwelcome publicity. The fact that Bird has not published anything makes it difficult to prove any offence.

Bird claims to have got back all manuscripts and tapes from Greenfield
(of John Farquharson Ltd, London literary agent) and Zwar and to have
rubbed out the tapes. Skoug (of German Affairs) was inclined to believe
that Greenfield had come clean if only because of Farquharson's reputation, but was more doubtful about Zwar. Zwar apparently said that he
had returned everything ... another letter has gone to him asking for
'everything *tout suite*'.

Rubbish! I had not sent anything back to the State Department, as requested
on the phone by a panicked Gene Bird. I had said to him that he could tell
the State Department I was not an American subject and would publish the
book in my own name, not his, and would not even mention him. What
Hess had to say was the salient point.

The British Embassy message stated: 'Bird is not to be trusted ... though
it could be reasonably hoped that he would not do anything until Hess had
died.' After that, reasoned the Embassy, any damage publication might do
would be limited.

By now Mr Basil Hall, MC, TD, Deputy Treasury Solicitor in Whitehall,
had been contacted by the Foreign Office for an expert opinion. What
could be done to stop the book's publication under the Official Secrets
Act, he was asked? Not a lot, he had replied (to Mr Rodney Batstone, Legal
Advisers Department in the Foreign Office). It seemed 'impractical' to rely
on section 2 of the 1911 Act, he said, because:

1. It seemed doubtful whether Spandau Prison could be a 'prohibited
   place' as defined by section 3 of the Act. It was difficult to argue that it
   belonged to or was occupied by or on behalf of Her Majesty.
2. Even if Spandau prison were a prohibited place, the section does not
   apply to Colonel Bird who committed no offence in any part of Her
   Majesty's dominions and is not a British officer or subject.
3. There is nothing which one can at present do to Greenfield or John
   Farquharson Ltd. They have not attempted to communicate the information.

We discussed whether there would be any point in writing to the publishers saying that publication might contravene the Official Secrets Act. I think we both hold the view that this might well prove an embarrassment, because there was no reason why the publishers should not make it public that they had received this message; even if we thought that a court might hold that there was a breach, which I for one do not; to write might be inadvisable.

Rodney Batstone of the FO wrote back:

Dear Basil, Many thanks for your letter. I am grateful for your help over this.

In the light of our discussion we have suggested that the Americans be advised to work on Bird who might be able to withdraw the copy from Greenfield. We must hope that this produces results.

George Greenfield had my manuscript in his office safe, and was to experience a sinister, bullying operation at the hands of Special Branch and the War Office, anxious to seize another secret and sensitive manuscript to prevent its publication. Greenfield had been called on by Superintendent Smith of the Special Branch who had threatened to 'turn over the author's drum' to get his hands on a book he had written.

'He was shortish and fat,' George recalled in his memoirs, *A Smattering of Monsters*, 'with a fair complexion roughened by a countryman's exposure to the sun and the wind and the rain. He had small eyes and his gaze slipped and slid around the room, looking for hiding places, assessing the contents, summing up the occupant's status. I had a packet of cigarettes on my desk, to which he kept on helping himself throughout the interview. He was egregiously, almost insolently, polite, wielding the word "sir" like a blackjack at the end of most sentences. Along with the obsequious tone, there was a phoney air of comradeship, verging on conspiracy. "You an' me, sir – we're men of the world, sir. We've seen most things in our time. We could be mates, except you're the officer class I can see, sir, and I'm another rank."'

He began by formally asking me to hand over the spare typescript. I said it was not in the office and asked him, as a matter of interest, what would happen if I refused to let it go.

'Oh, that wouldn't be clever, Sir. My word, no. You see, I'd have to get a warrant and bring in some of my men to search this office of yours. I have to tell you, Sir, these young fellas you get in the Force today – they're a clumsy bunch an' no mistake. They'd have to go through all your files – an' I expect you've got some real important ones here, Sir, your best authors an' all that. Could be they'd knock over a bottle of ink, right over those important files. Don't worry, Sir, I'd make 'em apologise to you – in person, like. But those files wouldn't look too good, no, sir.

'Another thing. Young coppers are so careless these days. They smoke like chimneys – oh thanks, Sir, don't mind if I do – an' they don't always stub the fags out proper. Leave 'em burning all over the place. Lot of wood round here, Sir, I can see. Make a real little blaze, that would!'

I reached for a cigarette from the rapidly diminishing packet and took my time lighting it. He was playing with me; he knew this game inside out from long practice – as he proved from his next remarks.

'You were in the forces, I reckon, Sir. You look a military gent, if I may say so. You remember that old saying, Sir, "You can't beat the army." Lots of squaddies tried but where did they end up? In the glasshouse, that's where. It's the same with us, Sir. Now I know your firm's got a daybook and a private ledger. It couldn't run without 'em. Under the terms of the warrant, I could impound 'em both. And, like I say, Sir, these fellas who work for me can be damn careless. Not the training we went through. Could be – I'm only saying "could be" – those vital files got mislaid or lost forever. Scotland Yard's like a bloody rabbit warren – excuse my language, Sir. Things go missing and never turn up again. Of course, you'd get a written apology from a very senior officer – maybe even a Deputy Assistant Commissioner – but it'd be difficult to run your business and hang on to those important clients without them ...'

(From George Greenfield's Memoir 'A Smattering of Monsters', published by Camden House; now out of print.)

By now the problem with the Bird-Zwar book had become a matter of international concern. Confidential telegrams were being sent between Washington, London and Berlin, copied to Bonn, Moscow and Paris embassies (but 'not passed to the French').

Colonel Bird, then under house arrest in Berlin, was reported to be

> reasonably cooperative, but not 100 per cent so. US Mission have recommended that he should be allowed to resign and return at an early date to Florida where his wife was very ill. [The] manuscript has not been fully checked by US Mission here [Berlin] yet. But it is known to discuss death arrangements and appears to draw on Quadripartite and Tripartite classified documents. [Interview with Hess] tapes are stated by Bird to be not in Berlin but in possession of Greenfield and Zwar. (Latter incidentally is said to live in Queensland and to be the author of *The Infamous of Nuremberg* in co-operation with an earlier US Colonel.)
>
> Hess appears to have happily co-operated on the basis that he was putting his historical record straight.
>
> US Mission claims that knowledge of this case is very closely restricted to a few people in Berlin and Washington, i.e. at present to no-one in the London Embassy.

In the meantime, what should the Americans do to Colonel Bird?

There were considerable bureaucratic complications in Washington, the telegrams said. And the British Embassy was made aware of the situation. One of their messages stated:

> US officials [are] reportedly divided between those who want to bring him home for the purpose of punishing him, and those who want to keep him in Berlin for the purpose of getting to the bottom of the whole story and neutralising the damage done. At present the latter view is prevailing. The Soviet Governor of Spandau is showing increasing interest in Bird's welfare and whereabouts. We have privately informed the Americans here that Major Yefremov had already appeared to be suspicious of Bird and had asked the British Governor a week or two earlier whether he thought Bird was helping Hess to write his memoirs.

> US Mission have also received information that the Australian named
> Zwar also operated under the name of 'Zwar Features' from an address at
> 65 Cadogan Gardens, SW3.

Weeks later, the British Embassy in Washington was reporting that Colonel
Bird (now in Washington) had summoned up enough courage 'to return to
the charge over the publication of his manuscript on Hess'.

> Having first approached the Pentagon, he was interviewed in the State
> Department the other day. Bird was asking for permission to publish.
> Exactly what he would publish was left obscure, since he maintains that
> he returned his only manuscript to the US authorities. He did not ask for
> it back ...

True. But as co-author of the book, I had my copy of the manuscript still
hidden in the brickwork of my Cairns, Queensland workshop, ready for
publication.

Col. Bird was informed, said the Embassy, that 'under current circumstances' there could be no question of his receiving permission to publish;
although if Hess should die or Spandau prison be closed down, he could
make formal application. It was felt better to leave him with the hope of
eventual permission. The reasoning behind this was that 'without such a
hope he might feel sufficiently frustrated to go ahead and publish now'.

Mr. M.L.H. Hope of the Embassy's Western European Department went
on: 'Although Bird denies having a manuscript, he claims to be able to
rewrite the book from memory. He nevertheless gave every assurance that
he would not publish now. Whether or not he is being honest in saying he
did not keep a copy of the manuscript (which one is entitled to doubt) it
seems pretty certain that Zwar, his collaborator in Australia, has one. Zwar
has also written asking for permission to publish, claiming that he, too,
could rewrite the book from memory if the manuscript were not returned.'
Again, not true. I had never claimed I had the capacity of committing to
memory 200,000 words.

Mr Hope continued: 'Since Zwar is only a ghost-writer and has no personal knowledge or access to Hess this is even less plausible than Bird's claim.'

No access to Hess? I had, by now, four years of access to Hess through my trained reporter, Colonel Bird. He had been air-mailing three or four cassette tapes every week, cleared by HM Customs in Cairns, with Rudolf Hess's answers to the questions I was asking and Hess's own pencilled annotations. At the time, I was sending back by return mail the chapters written from that information and Bird would take them into the prison for Hess to check. If the old man wished to work on them in the garden he would stuff the pages into his underpants and make his way to the garden seat where, under the noses of the sentinels in the guard towers, he would write his comments in the margins.

The State Department had forgotten, or was unaware of, the involvement in the saga of a VIP – America's own Secretary of State.

During Gene Bird's time as US Commandant at Spandau, he had a visit from an American official called Russell. Bird had phoned to tell me about it. 'Mr Russell told me in the strictest confidence that Henry Kissinger, Secretary of State, had sent him over to collaborate with me to write a book on Rudolf Hess! I told him I would have no part of it. He was out of order.' (Hess, while they were talking, had the latest chapter of my manuscript stuffed in his underpants to read in the garden.)

When the colonel was flown to Washington to appear before twelve of the Top Brass, there at the table was Russell. Bird told me he said: '"I know you, don't I, Mr Russell?"

'He looked at me: "I have never seen you before."'

✳✳✳

Forty years later – in July 2009 – through State Department retirement archives I found Mr Harold Russell. I put to him all that Gene Bird had told me when he went before a State Department Board to request the return of our seized manuscript and to obtain permission for its publication.

Eugene Bird said he would never forget his confrontation in Washington. He told me on the phone that he had asked to get his manuscript on Hess returned and to have permission to publish:

'I walked into the [Washington] meeting and there was Mr Russell, right in the middle of everybody. He was the international lawyer in charge of

European Affairs for the State Department while Henry Kissinger was Secretary of State. There were 7–9 people at the table. I went in and sat down. I had last seen Russell eighteen months before.

'I was a little frightened. Russell said: "Who are you?" I said: "My name is Bird." "Bird?" he said. "Never heard of you. What do you want?"

'"Sir, I am asking to get my manuscript back and I am asking permission to publish."

'"What d'you mean, 'manuscript'? About what?"

'"About Rudolf Hess in Spandau. I have a question, Sir. Mr Russell, were you not in my office?"

'Russell then said: "Wait a minute! Wait a minute! When the balloon goes up you can get in here and see about getting your manuscript back."

'I said: "Now you know who I am and you know about the manuscript. I am going to leave this room right now and go back to my room in the Mayflower Hotel and I am going to start to write another book; standing on my rights of freedom of speech."

'Russell then said: "You had better watch out, Bird, or you're gonna end up in prison yourself!"

'I said: "I'm going to take that chance" and walked out and closed the door.'

Eugene Bird later wrote about his experience to Wolf-Rudiger Hess:

In December, 1972, I appeared in front of a Board of officers in the State Department in Washington DC. My reason for appearing there was to retrieve my manuscript. I was denied this, even though a member of the panel – a Mr Russell – had been in my office in West Berlin and had himself tried to influence me to write a book about your Father, for the State Department.

He wrote to me:

At this time, Mr Russell – the lawyer (the one who spoke to me about writing in Spandau) – stated: 'Don't give up hope – come in after (Hess's) death or closure (of the prison) and talk further. I won't say exactly what, but feel something can be worked out.'

That was the only bright spot (hope) in the meeting.

Bird told our literary agent George Greenfield:

> I was encouraged by a high official from the State Department in Washington DC to get as much information from Hess as I could ... as it was felt in Washington that I was the only one who could do it. My relationship with the prisoner was widely known, not only in Berlin but also in Washington.
>
> My mistake was in the fact that I did not tell him that I had already written a manuscript.

(Col. Bird's revelation that his relationship with Hess was 'widely known' in both Berlin and Washington dismayed me – his co-author. It seemed that since we had last met, he had become a loose cannon, which was under-lined by him taking a camera into Spandau to film Hess. I had no idea he was going to do it and the escapade had never been part of our collaboration; nor did I share in any payment for television usage which goes on to this day.)

Col. Bird had been billeted at the Mayflower Hotel in Virginia Gate, Washington DC, where – a few months before – five of President Richard Nixon's henchmen were arrested for breaking into the headquarters of the Democratic National Committee.

He wrote to me: 'I fear [there has been] censorship of my and your letters. My writing this book has done so much for history ...'

He then air-mailed a fifteen-page letter to Greenfield in London, which said (among other things) that he believed a 'leak' in the studios and offices of London's ITN had led to his arrest; his State Department inquisitors had described in detail what was on the film he had shot and specifically what was on many of the tapes he had sent me.

> My losses amount to some $US17,000 a year, plus many advantages, which add up to about $US20,000 a year. I run the chance of loss of pension, rights which could run into many, many thousands; not to mention a business in occupied Berlin (a paint factory).

I am in great sympathy with Desmond, whom I consider to be one of my best friends; I miss terribly working with him on our great and important (to history) work.

1. All manuscript, pictures, negatives, translations, back-up material, documents, copies, signatures etc have been impounded. I had to turn over all material. Not to have done so would have been to tell a lie. The investigation and interrogation were very complete. I was under oath.

2. There were four more copies made of all manuscripts. The three I turned over (your copy, Desmond's copy and mine), made seven in all.

Col. Bird was told copies were to be sent to the US Commander in Berlin, the Head of Mission in Berlin, one to the US Embassy in Bonn, 'and I believe four copies were sent on to Washington DC to be examined by various levels of departments of Government – I can only guess – to Department of State, Department of Defense etc.'

3. All back-up material; i.e. documents, papers, letters, pictures, statements, tapes etc are sealed in a metal container and locked in a secret vault under absolute control in Berlin.

4. There was a very thorough investigation conducted by the US Army and State Department. It lasted over a month ... and is still going on. I was not represented by an attorney, as I was investigated only. If I am to be tried I will of course have an attorney.

5. I was dismissed from my job at Spandau and <u>will never return.</u>

6. I was told to be silent on the question of Spandau. Keen interest was placed on this ... so as not to embarrass the US, its Allies and generally make things worse at the prison for the old man.

7. Both Desmond's name and yours were brought into the picture; your background and your reputation. Both were found to be outstanding. ... I have reason to believe the British Government was more than likely brought into the picture, perhaps the Australian (Government) also. I believe counter-espionage efforts were brought into play. I do know all mail, phone-calls etc were checked and no doubt still are being watched and checked.

I well expected to be taken into custody when I arrived in the US; this has not happened as yet. I have not been 'charged' with an offense. The investigation is still going on. They are of course aware of Desmond and his part in the book. Desmond is not bound to the US Government in any way, but he is to [our] contract. I had to sign the Secrets Act which has been made much stronger since the Vietnam Papers Affair. I had many talks with Desmond and we decided to go with it and run the risk. We both felt, as we all feel now, that we were doing something good for history. It was the [ITN] film that broke the camel's back.

You may rest assured that both Des and I are being carefully watched. [The Americans' visit to my cellar had confirmed he was correct.]

Again from the Mayflower he wrote on 13 November 1972, to Lt. Col. F.B. Reed, Chief of the News Branch of the Public Information Division, Department of the Army, making these points:

I have submitted all material to the United States Headquarters in Berlin. The manuscript is approx. 160,000 words. It was in a near-finished state – missing the last chapter yet to be written.

A tentative title *The Loneliest Man in the World* had been chosen – *the inside story of Spandau Prison and its lone prisoner, Rudolf Hess.*

I stress that the manuscript has in no way been written for the sake of sensation, nor in any way that could be damaging to any one person or nation.

Extensive and exhaustive research has gone into the manuscript over many years ... and has been written for the sake of history. It is factual. It tells it exactly as it was and is!

I believe that I have grown to know and understand Rudolf Hess better than any living person since his flight in 1941. He has willingly given me answers to questions that historians have been seeking for years. He has given me exclusive rights (permission) to publish all or part of his former letters, diaries, speeches and documents, provided exact translations were made.

Some statements he volunteered to me when he lay close to death (when he thought he would die) in his cell and in hospital, as I sat as the only person at his bedside. I should like to state that I considered it my duty to write the manuscript and was encouraged to do so, over the years, by many of my superiors in West Berlin.

I submitted my manuscript when it was more than three-fourths finished, to the US Commander in Berlin's Chief-of-Staff for review.

I was told such things as 'well-written', 'excellent', 'factual', 'important to history', 'stirring', 'revealing', 'continue with your writing'. I was encouraged to get as much information as I could from the prisoner. I did it.

Col. Bird then spoke about a superior officer's encouragement to go on writing in case Hess died or the prison was shut down. He said the manuscript was in this man's possession for ten days and that Bird 'had every reason to believe he had shown it to the then United States Commander of Berlin'. He continued:

I had secured a co-author, Mr Desmond Zwar, who had written a book with a Col. Burton C. Andrus (USA Ret.), the former US Commandant of the prison holding all of the major war criminals in Nuremberg, Germany, prior to and during the war trials conducted by the Military Tribunal. He was able to furnish me much valuable and factual background information. He is also an historian and a recognized author with excellent writing style. I had also secured a leading literary agent. I entered into a contract with Mr Zwar which states that the manuscript would not be released for publication unless there was a signed agreement by both parties. Further, responsibility rested with me to obtain approval from Washington D.C. for publication of the book.

My book does not violate any security regulations, nor is it offensive to any one persona or nation. It covers an important gap in history … it answers questions – with the help of Hess – which leading historians have been asking for years. It would have been good if a recorder had been with Napoleon in his last days and had taken down his spoken word.

He handed over a statement he had prepared outlining his years of collaboration with the prisoner, Hess.

I have been asked by many people, my superiors in Berlin – people have said, 'you should write a book one day and tell the TRUE story.'

It is something that should be recorded for the sake of history. There have been speculations in newspapers and magazines in every language in the world of what is going on [in the prison]. They have said, 'here is a madman being kept in chains and starved'; or 'here is a man living off the fat of the land.' It has been speculation because nobody knew what was going on. If Hess died tomorrow and no one had taken the trouble to set down the true, factual record proved by documentation of medical and psychiatric reports, first-hand conversations with Hess … the true story would never be told. The question-mark over Spandau would remain … Were they being cruel to Hess? Humane to Hess? Was he mad?

I am trying to show the world, with the help of Hess himself, what was really behind his flight and what went on in his inner-thinking.

I became more convinced than ever that I must write this book after Speer and von Schirach were released at the end of September 1966; when Hess was left in the prison alone, practically in solitary confinement. He was not sentenced to that.

Hess has been called the most examined man in the world, medically and physically. If you have some 200 psychiatrists over the years, come to try and understand you, it must have some effect on you … as a result he has withdrawn more and more into his shell where he lives. Many have thought, and still think, he is insane. In my many hours of talking to him, reading letters he has written etc., I have found him to be an intelligent man. What he did in flying to England was, indeed, no simple thing.

I have come close to the answer of Hess because I have taken the trouble to talk to Hess – not as someone who has come to examine him – but as close to the man as my job would permit so Hess could talk to me normally.

I have faithfully recorded these conversations. If I were trying to put anything into them or subtract anything from them, I would, like the rest, be trying to read things into what he says – as a psychiatrist. I am therefore trying to report as a reporter, what he has said to me in his cell, in walks in the garden and when he lay close to death in hospital. I have come to know him, I believe, better than any living person since 1941.

My book is the story of a man who helped start a war, who once vainly tried to stop it, and who now lives in virtual solitary confinement in a prison.

Eugene K. Bird.

In a further statement, he said to a Dr Mundt of the German publishing house that was considering the book: 'It was Mr Hess himself who often prompted me to write a book. He used to read articles written about him – also books – many of which printed non-truths about him. "Lies!" he used to tell me. "Here I am, in prison, and unable to correct them!"'

Prior to obtaining permission from Mr. Zwar to aid in writing the book, I had to present Mr. Zwar with proof that Mr. Hess would give his permission and would co-operate. This was done in a short letter exchanged between Mr. Zwar and Mr. Hess. I smuggled Mr. Hess's reply of assurance (letter of permission) from Mr. Hess to Mr. Zwar. Only then would Mr. Zwar co-operate in writing the book.

Col. Bird wrote a week later to George Greenfield that he had endured 'extreme and exhaustive' interviews with the Department of Defence and was scheduled to go before a State Department Board.

I feel that I won them [Defence officials] on many points … they seemed to be fascinated about the book, though they perhaps were not supposed to approach it in this manner. The big, big test will come on Friday. I know they are beefing up for me and may even fly people in from West Berlin. The State Department seems to be hostile …

Gene Bird may indeed have put on a brave face to George Greenfield. But his immediate letter to me as he emerged from the State Department grilling the same day was somewhat different. He wrote on 29 November 1972, from his room at the down-at-heel Mayflower Hotel, hours after the confrontation:

It would be cruel of me not to keep you posted as soon as possible.

It is now 2330 hours and I have had exhausting interviews with the highest-level officials in the Pentagon. I saw the letter you wrote to Mr Donohue ... also met and discussed with great length, the entire book. I layed all – I repeat all – on the open table and delivered my level best as if on world-wide TV. I felt their response in my very nerve center! My months and months of training, using auto suggestion and cosmic habit force – the power of thought – really paid off today.

The big test is yet to come. I received a great deal of encouragement from the Department of the Army. But the State Department is the big test. I believe your masterly letter to Donohue helped immensely.

I had written to Mr Donohue at the State Department immediately after Col. Bird's arrest:

I wish to open with you a sensible discussion on the book's future. I have worked for four years on an unsensational, honest and utterly accurate book which, during production, was seen, read and approved by at least two Generals in Berlin. Col. Bird was actively encouraged to write down the history of Spandau and most particularly, to record his dialogues with Hess, which are of great historic value and which contain valuable information which might otherwise die with him. You will no doubt be aware that I am an Australian citizen and do not come under your Department's jurisdiction regarding the publication or otherwise of what I have written. I fully understand the embarrassment that could be caused if such a book were published under Col. Bird's name during Hess's confinement; and despite most attractive financial offers, have fully kept my word with Col. Bird that only he can give any go-ahead for publication after the manuscript has been cleared by yourselves. Accordingly I have now re-written this manuscript under my own name, removing the Foreword and Col. Bird's name, and every reference to the First Person in the book (i.e. his direct statements like 'Hess told me'). I therefore now would like to put it to you that I see no reason for not publishing the manuscript in its re-written form – with the removal of the chapter on the future of the prisoner's body (the only chapter that could cause embarrassment to another nation). I should therefore like to have direct communication with yourself, so that a cool and reasoned discussion can take place between us. I could not lightly allow four years' work to be destroyed by a 'freezing' of this book, without good reason.

Gene Bird had returned from Florida (where his wife remained ill) to Washington to plead for the release of our book for publication. But the State Department was digging in its heels.

I then received a reply from Francis W. Tully, Office of Policy and Plans, Bureau of Public Affairs at the State Department:

I refer to your letter concerning the manuscript on Spandau Prison and Rudolph [sic] Hess of which you advise me you are the co-author and in which you state that only LTC Bird can give the go-ahead for publication after authorization by the United States Department of State.

Such authorization has neither been requested or granted. The changes and deletions you state you have made in this manuscript do not alter the requirement that authorization to publish be first obtained from the Department of State.

I replied to Mr Tully:

I received your letter ... with some dismay. You state that ... only LTC Bird can give the go-ahead for publication after authorisation by the United States Department of State. And that 'such authorisation by the State Department has neither been requested nor granted'.

I have been informed specifically that such authorisation was asked for, both verbally and in writing. Indeed, I have a photocopy of the letter written by LTC Bird before he left on this one mission: to have permission for publication now or in the specific future. And LTC Bird, who I have always trusted implicitly, gave me, as my right, a full and verbatim report of what happened at the meeting at which you, yourself, were present.

I am upset that you have taken such an aloof attitude towards my seeking a sensible dialogue and to write to me something which, to say the very least, is an insult to my gullibility.

Why, otherwise, than wishing to see the fruition of so many years' work, encouraged by your own general staff, would Col. Bird have made the journey to Washington if it was not to seek information on the future of this book?

I said that the manuscript in its present form (*The Loneliest Man in the World*, by Eugene K. Bird, Former US Director of Spandau) could be scrapped and I would re-write it and publish it in my own name as the story of Hess's life in prison since 1941, without reference to Eugene Bird in any way. 'It pains me,' I said, 'to have to act in this way after being indirectly encouraged by the highest US officials in Berlin to do the honest research and writing that all of us hoped would be a history the US might be proud of.'

A few days later I had a phone call from Gene which this time was obviously not supervised. He seemed far more relaxed. A US publisher who had a copy of our manuscript had been telephoned by the Berlin Desk of the CIA and told to 'let things simmer down'. A show of indignation by the Americans was being put on for the Soviets. We could publish later, in the form the book was now in. 'Please make sure Zwar doesn't change anything.'

The Loneliest Man in the World was finally published in twelve countries and serialised in newspapers and magazines. But it did not result in Hess's release, despite the sympathy it aroused worldwide. The Russians refused to budge.

There was still one moral task left that we owed to Rudolf Hess. I had kept his diaries and his manifesto pecked out by him on an old typewriter in Nuremberg prison. To make sure they would not be seized if ever we were found out, Eugene Bird had entrusted me with them; they had remained behind the false bricks in my workshop, gathering dust, for fourteen years. Now it was time to return them to the family.

I extracted them from my workshop brickwork and flew back with them in a hand-held briefcase from Cairns to Munich. Gene Bird met me and we took a taxi out to Wolf-Rudiger's home, handing him the 500 pages of Hess's handwritten diary, giving the authentic insight into the mind of the world's strangest old man. Hess Jr was close to tears when he opened the package. (So were Eugene Bird and I, but for a different reason. A collector of Nazi memorabilia, hearing we had the archive, had offered us $US250,000 for it a few days earlier. We turned him down.)

Bird had earlier written to Hess Jr, outlining his association with his father and the book resulting from the collaboration. He revealed that indeed there had been three cardboard cartons handed to him for destruction as being of no further use following the Nuremberg Tribunal – one marked 'Hess', another 'von Schirach' and the third 'Speer'.

They had been screened from the Nazi Archives here in Berlin by officials, believing they were just a collection of private scribblings and, believing that all had been put on micro-film, gave these boxes to me to burn if I wanted. For three years I left the boxes unopened. One night I did open them and found many papers from the people tried at Nuremberg, and the prisoners of Spandau Prison, including your father.

I told Mr Hess what I had found and he was impatient to examine the papers. I had often spoken to your father about his responsibility to write for history. He agreed to this, but always stated that his memory was not good enough.

After the discovery of the cartons and his papers in them, your father told me: 'I give you permission to publish them in full or in part; I only ask that in the translation nothing in the sense of what I have written be altered.'

I promised that only an academic translator would be used. Through Mr Zwar a Dr Arengo-Jones, senior language superior of the BBC, was contracted.

I transferred all information to tape cassettes and then the words were typed by Mrs and Mr Zwar and put into the form of a manuscript.

As soon after typing as possible, I would take the type-written pages to your father (often together with original writings of his) and he was allowed to have them in his cell for sometimes up to 48 hours.

All of this was done at great risk. Therefore we proceeded as rapidly as possible. In addition to my written notes, I also had Mr Hess speak on toneband [tape] for as many as six hours. Here he answered important questions or simply talked at length about certain subjects (mainly what he described was his 'peace flight' or 'mission' to Scotland).

Later on I filmed him on 8 mm film in his cell and in the prison garden – altogether about 29 minutes. Much of this film was done with him talking at the same time on tape-recorder. These 29 minutes were later reduced to nine minutes with added sound effects. Mr Hess was able to review much of this film in its raw form before editing.

As the manuscript neared completion, Mr Hess saw and read every page, except that portion concerning the death of a prisoner in Spandau. After reading and making corrections on the original copy of the manuscript, Mr Hess initialled the upper right corner of each page with R.H.

In July 2009, retired lawyer Harold Russell identified himself as the lawyer for the State Department's European Bureau, who visited Spandau prison in December 1971, and met Col. Bird.

He told me: 'I had just joined the Department and was making a tour of the important posts in Germany. Dr Kissinger, later Secretary of State, had nothing to do with my visit and certainly did not convey a message of any kind through me to Col. Bird. I certainly did not encourage Col. Bird to write the book, which was totally unauthorized, and against the prison's regulations, since, as I recall, no prisoner was to be interviewed without representatives of all Four Powers present. The Department concluded that the book contained no new information about Hess and therefore decided not to take any action in opposition to its publication.'

Mr Russell said he was present 'at a hearing of sorts' to consider permission for the book to be published. He denies that he told Col. Bird that he had 'never seen him before'.

He went on: 'Bird's fantastic description of the meeting in Washington is truly amusing. He could not possibly have simply remembered the event incorrectly. Those present had read (or looked over) his manuscript before the meeting, so the idea that we did not know who he was or why he was there is laughable.'

Eugene Bird's closest friend in Berlin, Mr Bob Bakke, argues with the lawyer's version. He told me: 'Eugene K. Bird on several occasions told me about this bizarre experience with Mr Russell – it really disturbed him all his life. He felt betrayed by his own countrymen. He was under house arrest. Eight or nine boxes of documents had been confiscated from his house. On 26 April 1972, he was relieved of his position as Governor of Spandau prison.

'I didn't know Eugene in 1971–1972, but 20 years later he told me more than once about this visit of Mr Russell, where he shared current data and dreams to publish a historical book about Rudolf Hess and his mysterious flight. Mr Russell (an American official) wanted to know everything and encouraged Eugene to keep writing about the history of Rudolf Hess.'

CHAPTER 18

HE WAS MURDERED!

I n 1987 Hess, blind in one eye, shuffling around with the aid of a stick, and in pain from an enlarged prostate, had hidden himself from the eyes of sentries in the prison towers, wrapped an electric flex round his neck, pulled it tight and hanged himself.

That was the official suicide story. But Bird, who still had close ties to prison officials who were there during his command and after he left, told me on the phone that he believed Hess was murdered.

He walked with a cane, dragging his right foot behind him, because he had suffered a slight stroke. He was blind in the right eye and could see very little out of the left eye. Whenever he walked in the garden, he had to have a man on each side, in case he stumbled and fell. Hess could not tie his own shoes, his hands suffered so badly from arthritis. He could not get his fingers and thumbs apart, they had to literally insert a spoon into his hand so he could eat.

Most significant about whether he suicided or not is the fact that he could not raise his arms above shoulder level. To hang yourself, you have to be able to do that. Yet, with all his disabilities, a 93-year-old man, a prisoner watched more closely than any other in history, at a massive cost each year, was said to have entered the garden hut alone, tied an electric flex round his neck, looped it over a hatch just 1 m 30 cm from the floor

— not high enough to hang a cat — and strangled himself! The flex of the standard lamp actually remained in the wall socket.

Col. Bird said to me that Hess's male nurse, Mr Abdallah Melaouhi, had pushed his way to the death scene 'despite strenuous efforts to keep him away. He got to the scene within minutes. He says he saw a black American guard, excited, sweating and with his tie awry, shouting: "The pig is finished!" That guard has avoided all attempts to interview him. When a television crew approached him to talk he ran away.' Mr Melaouhi told an inquest on Hess's death:

I, ABDALLAH MELAOUHI, of [address] do solemnly and sincerely declare as follows:

I worked as a male nurse caring for Rudolf Hess from 1 August 1982 until his death on 17 August 1987 at the Allied Military Prison in Spandau. From 1967 to 1970 I trained as a technical medical assistant in tropical diseases at the Institute of Tropical Medicine in Hamburg. From 1970, I continued my training as a qualified male nurse until 1973 when I received a Diploma Certificate in Nursing. In 1974 I moved to Berlin and worked at Hohengatow Hospital in the intensive care unit until 1976. I then attended the specialist medical school, Gauschule, Wedding, at the recommendation of the Department of Health at the Berlin Senate until 1977 and upon completing that training I received a Diploma in anaesthesia and the intensive care of sick people. I was then promoted to Superior Male Nurse and went to work at Spandau Hospital (Krankenhaus, Spandau) in the intensive care unit until 1st August 1982 when I went to work in the Allied Military Prison in Spandau as Male Nurse for Rudolf Hess.

On the day of Mr Hess's death, 17 August 1987, I commenced my duties, which involved caring for Mr Hess, as usual at 6.45 a.m. I assisted him, as was usual, with showering and dressing, and was present when he ate a meal at 10.30 a.m. At no time did he give any indication that his state of mind was disturbed or that he was unduly depressed.

Shortly after the meal, he asked me to go to the nearby town of Spandau to purchase a ceramic pot to replace one which was defective. Mr Hess would not have made such a request merely to ensure my absence, since I was always absent in any event from midday, during my noon pause.

At 2 p.m. I was called to the prison from my flat which was located outside, but in the immediate vicinity of, the prison (to which I had gone on my return from the town of Spandau).

After some delay I reached the summerhouse in the prison garden where I was told that there had been an incident. The small door at the front of the summerhouse was closed. When I entered the summerhouse, the scene was like a wrestling match had taken place; the entire place was in confusion. The straw tiled mat which covered the floor was in disarray, although only the day before I had cleaned the floor and had left the straw tiled mat carefully arranged in its usual place. A tall lamp had fallen over, but I clearly remember that the cable attached to the lamp was still connected to the main socket. It was this lamp cable which the authorities later said that Mr Hess had used to hang himself. A round table and Mr Hess's armchair had also been overturned. In summary, none of the furniture or equipment was in its usual place, and there is no question in my mind but that a struggle had taken place in the summerhouse.

The body of Mr Hess was lying on the floor of the summerhouse, apparently lifeless. Near to his body stood two soldiers dressed in US Army uniforms. I had never seen either soldier before. I also saw an American guard, whom I knew as a Mr Tony Jordan. There was no cable anywhere near the body of Mr Hess; as I have said, the only cable was attached to the fallen lamp which was still plugged into the wall. I immediately proceeded to examine Mr Hess. I could not detect any respiration, pulse or heartbeat. I estimated that death had occurred 30 to 40 minutes earlier.

The guard whom I knew as Jordan stood near Mr Hess's feet and appeared overwrought. He was sweating heavily, his shirt was saturated with sweat and he was not wearing a tie. I said to Jordan: 'what have you done with him?' He replied: 'The pig is finished, you won't have to work a night shift any longer.' I told him to bring the emergency case (which contained a first aid kit) and the oxygen appliance, while I commenced artificial respiration. When Jordan returned with the equipment, I noticed that he had first taken the opportunity to change his clothes. The equipment which he brought had clearly been interfered with. The seal on the emergency case had been broken open and its contents were in a state of disorder. The intubation instrument set had no battery and the tube was perforated. Further, the oxygen appliance had no oxygen in it. Yet when I had checked the emergency case and the oxygen appliance that same morning, as part of my normal duties, I am certain that both had been in full working order. Since I did not have any of the necessary equipment I did the best I could which was to perform mouth to mouth resuscitation on Mr Hess and I asked one of the soldiers in American uniform to conduct a heart massage on him. This was at approximately 3.20 p.m. These efforts had no discernable effect. A doctor and a medical orderly whom I did not recognise arrived from the English Military Hospital in an ambulance. They brought a heart-lung machine into the summerhouse. I tried to operate the machine but it did not appear to function. Mr Hess was taken to hospital. I accompanied him and made further unsuccessful attempts to resuscitate him in the ambulance. There were final unsuccessful attempts to resuscitate him by the doctors at the hospital. He was pronounced dead at the hospital at 16.10 hours.

During the five years in which I daily cared for Mr Hess, I was able to obtain a clear and accurate impression of his physical capabilities. I do not consider, given his physical condition, that it would have been possible for Mr Hess to have committed suicide in the manner later published by the Allied powers. He had neither the strength nor the mobility to place an electric flex around his neck, knot it and either hang or strangle himself. Mr Hess was so weak that he needed a special chair to help him stand up. … Most significantly, his hands were crippled with arthritis; he was not able, for example, to tie his shoelaces. I consider that he was incapable of the degree of manual dexterity necessary to manipulate the electric flex as suggested.

Further, he was not capable of lifting his arms above his shoulders; it is therefore in my view not possible that he was able to attach the electric flex to the window catch from which he is alleged to have suspended himself.

Having regard to first Mr Hess's physical condition; second, the scene which I discovered in the summerhouse, in particular the location of the electric flex; and third, the surrounding circumstances as I have described them, I am firmly of the view that Mr Hess could not possibly have committed suicide as has been claimed.

In my view, it is clear that he met his death by strangulation, at the hands of a third party.

[signature of Abdallah Melaouhi]

[handwritten 17.2.1994. Qualification of person or officer taking the declaration: Reinhard Gizinski, Notary Public, Berlin.]

On the anniversary of Rudolf Hess's death, I phoned his son, Wolf-Rudiger Hess. We had met twice before: once while dining in Munich; and once when Bird and I, some years later, had given him tapes and typed documents Hess had written in Nuremberg prison.

Hess Jnr had spent his adult life fighting for his father's release and hinting that his continued incarceration involved secrets the Allies feared he would disclose about a British-Nazi 'connection' if he were set free.

I asked Wolf-Rudiger if he believed his father had taken his own life.

'He was murdered – by the SAS,' said Hess over the line to Australia.

'I am working even more intensely to prove that my father was strangled in that garden hut. And to prove that the British were behind it. I am absolutely convinced my father did not commit suicide by tying a lamp cord around his neck. There was a murder.'

Why had it happened?

The Russians, said Hess, were about to finally abandon their veto on his father's release, after forty-six years of stubbornly rejecting pleas by the other three powers – France, the US and Britain – to allow him to go home to his wife. Wolf had been called to the Soviet Embassy and informed of this.

'That meant that the Western powers could no longer hide behind the Russian veto. They never really wanted him released. So it was better to blame the Russians. They were quite sure the Russians would always say no. In fact they would not have been very happy if he was released.'

Did he believe he knew the reason for British reluctance to have Hess freed?

'Obviously he knew things they did not want to come out. You must not forget that the British government is keeping classified documents about my father secret until 2017. So it didn't make sense to have these documents kept secret and then release the crown witness.'

'I have spent years investigating what was in those documents, who they were embarrassing to and why. And it has been very difficult because the Allies try and block everything.

'They have destroyed the so-called suicide electric cable; they have destroyed the garden hut and the prison itself; all the details and the circumstances which could have led to finding out what really happened.

'The Allies have their reasons not to continue investigations. Scotland Yard started an investigation and gave a recommendation soon afterwards for a full-scale murder investigation. Then the Director of Public Prosecutions, Mr Green, said it was not necessary to continue.

'Obviously that decision was made by the government, Mrs Margaret Thatcher.'

In Berlin, Col. Eugene Bird had been investigating Hess's death – by talking to warders and officers then working in the prison and specifically to Hess's male nurse, Mr Abdallah Melaouhi.

'Hess was murdered,' said Gene Bird. 'I am convinced of it. The man was 93 years old. He could not even rise from a bench alone, he had to be helped up. He could not walk down the spiral staircase from his cell to the garden, they had to put in a lift in 1981, when he was in his late 80s.

'There were two other people there [at the scene] in American uniforms. Abdallah had never seen them before. He gave Hess mouth-to-mouth resuscitation, and when that failed he went to the resuscitation equipment which he had checked and signed as in good order just hours before – and found the oxygen tank empty and the tubes for breathing full of holes.

'Abdallah made a report and sent it to Scotland Yard. He has since had threats of death and is a scared man.'

Col. Bird concluded: 'If that man was murdered it had to be a decision taken at the highest level. I will say no more than that.'

A few minutes after my phone call to Col. Bird, I called Abdallah Melaouhi at his home in Berlin, where he had just returned after hospital duty. He said to me: 'Yes, I believe Mr Hess was murdered. But please … not on the telephone. You come to Berlin and see me. But not the telephone.'

Melaouhi had repeated his official statement to the world's media and, living 10,000 miles away in Australia, I realised a trip to see him in Berlin would add little.

THE LAST BIRD INTERVIEW

I n his last in-depth interview before he died, Colonel Eugene Bird spent an hour with Russian TV correspondent Serge Morozov at Bird's Berlin home.

Morozov says: 'It is important to realise that Col. Bird was recalling to me what Hess actually told him – not relating bits of history. He was very emotional at times, remembering his conversations with Hess.

'We taped the interview without interruptions – apart from Col. Bird taking a sip of tea while we changed the cassettes. And I have no reason not to believe he was telling me what Hess actually said.

'He was recollecting things that he hadn't talked about for some time and those meetings with Hess remained emotionally charged in his mind.'

On Hess's alleged suicide, Bird was unequivocal: 'Hess was ninety-three. He could not get up from a bench without help; he walked with a cane … he was recovering from a stroke and was blind in his right eye … He could not raise his arms to shoulder level … *And he hanged himself?*'

'What kind of a man was Hess?'

'Very difficult. Pulled back. I felt very uneasy around him; but I had great respect for his courage and his discipline. I believe there were still unanswered questions about his flight. Hess had great respect for England. He had praise for the English people and for their civilisation. He had little respect for Winston Churchill and told me that one of the conditions he had brought with him in 1941 was that the British Prime Minister be sacked!

'If Britain did not accede to his demands,' he recalled, 'Germany would order a land [sic] and sea blockade of Britain, throttling the country and starving its people.

'When at Dunkirk with 50,000 [sic] British soldiers with their backs to the sea, Hess recalled that he had stood at the right hand side of Hitler when Hitler ordered that they should not be attacked; that not a shot be fired.

'I asked Hess about this and his flight over many hours. I would then leave him and put everything on the tape recorder; memorising all of what was said.

'He agreed – in writing – that I could have access to all his writings, his speeches, his letters.'

Hess's son, Wolf-Rudiger Hess, says in his memoir *My Father, Rudolf Hess* that he wanted to see the document of exclusive copyright said to have been given by his father to Bird. But when he eventually saw a photocopy its quality was poor. When he visited his father, just prior to the book's publication in 1974, Hess had 'implored' him to prevent Bird's book appearing.

Col. Bird told Morozov that he had broached the sensitive question of Barbarossa, the German attack on Russia, asking: 'Mr Hess, did you help plan this attack? Were you on the planning committee?'

'Yes, yes, yes!' replied Hess testily.

But next day when Bird again brought up the subject, he said: 'No! I didn't know a thing about it.'

Having been assured by Hess that he would truthfully co-operate with Eugene Bird to write his book, Bird recalled: 'Finally I said to him, "Mr Hess, if you put this whole thing into a corner of your mind you will just be a laughing stock. Unless you cooperate with me; unless you give me your word with a handshake, that you will cooperate with me in writing our book together, it will come to nothing."

'He agreed and we shook hands.'

They were walking in the garden one day and the moon was still up. Hess pointed to it and said: 'Col. Bird, is it really true that the Americans have landed a man on the moon?' Afterwards, Hess was given moon charts and details of the moon landing which he hung on the walls of his cell.

On another walk, Bird wondered if Hess would still have chosen to serve a man like Adolf Hitler and consequently find himself serving a life sentence in prison.

There was a long silence. Then he said (after I counted about 200 steps), 'I once served under the greatest man who was born under the sun on this earth – der Führer. I would change nothing! I did the best I could for my country.'

I replied: 'Mr Hess, I am shocked! Aren't you sorry for what happened to the Jews?'

There was another long silence, then he said: 'Yes, I am sorry about that – but I was not in Germany at that time. I was a prisoner in England.'

'But you signed the Nuremberg Pact and the anti-Jewish Race Pact?'

'Yes, I signed,' said Hess.

Bird described Hess as 'extremely arrogant at times', and he 'felt uneasy about him'. Visited by a US general, Hess *demanded* (not asked) to be found not guilty of any crime. If that did not happen, said Hess, and even if the gates of Spandau were swung open for him, he would remain in his cell.

Col. Eugene Bird died aged 79, in Berlin, on 28 October 2005.

Desmond Zwar is the only reporter in the world to have secret access to two American prison governors guarding Hitler's jailed Nazi colleagues. He worked as a literary partner with Colonel Burton C. Andrus, Governor of Nuremberg prison, whose job was to keep behind bars twenty-four of Hitler's henchmen facing indictments for which many of them would hang. He then persuaded Colonel Eugene K. Bird, the US Commandant of Spandau prison, to secretly collaborate with Rudolf Hess and himself and document Hess's day-to-day prison life over a period of five years; including smuggling Zwar into Hess's cell.

INDEX